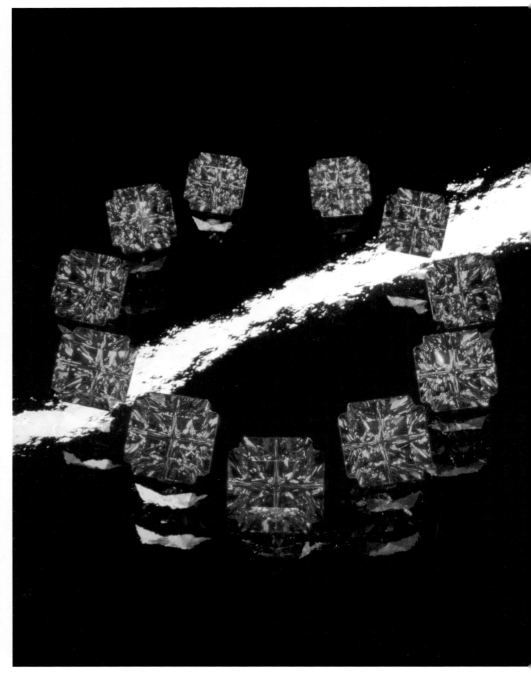

Above: Spessartine suite cut by Larry Woods of Jewels by Woods. *Photo by John Parrish.*

Opposite page: Serbian green opals (18.80 cts) with garnet, tourmaline and peridot accents. *Earrings designed and crafted by Paula Crevoshay. Photo by Chris Chavez.*

Exotic Gems

Volume 2

How to Identify and Buy
Alexandrite, Andalusite, Chrysoberyl Cat's-eye, Kyanite, Common Opal, Fire Opal, Dinosaur Gembone, Tsavorite, Rhodolite & Other Garnets

Renée Newman

International Jewelry Publications
Los Angeles _____

International Jewelry Publications
P.O. Box 13384
Los Angeles, CA 90013-0384 USA

(Inquiries should be accompanied by a self-addressed, stamped envelope.)

Printed in Singapore

Library of Congress Cataloging-in-Publication Data

Newman, Renée.
  Exotic Gems / Renée Newman.
      p. cm. – (Newman exotic gem series)
  Includes bibliographical references and index.
    ISBN-13: 978-0-929975-42-9 (trade pbk. : alk. paper)
1. Precious stones–Purchasing. 1. Title.
  TS752.N445 2010
  553.8--dc22

                                        2009037682

Front cover photos:
Fire opals and water opal from Emil Weis Opals. *Photo by Tanja Schütz.*
Tsavorite ring from Hubert, Inc. *Photo by Diamond Graphics.*
Kyanite from Stone Group Laboratories. *Photo by Bear Williams.*
Gembone ring from Different Seasons Jewelry. *Photo by David Greene.*
Rhodolite carved by Sherris Cottier Shank. *Photo by Amy Balthrop.*
Andalusite and photo from Coast-to-Coast Rare Gemstones.
Cat's-eye alexandrite from Pala International. *Photo: Wimon Manorotkul*

Spine: Earring by Paula Crevoshay. *Photo by Chris Chavez.*

Back cover: Spessartines cut by Larry Woods. *Photo by John Parrish.*

Contents

Acknowledgments

I would like to express my appreciation to the following people for their contribution to *Exotic Gems, Volume 2*:

Ernie and Regina Goldberger of the Josam Diamond Trading Corporation. This book could never have been written without the experience and knowledge I gained from working with them.

Mineralogist John S. White. He has edited a major portion of *Exotic Gems*. His recommendations and corrections have greatly improved this book.

Juan José Virgen Alatorre, Mark Anderson, John Bradshaw, Jessica Dow, John Dyer, Elaine Ferrari, Wolf Kuehn, Dean Lange, Bill Larson, Jürgen Schütz, Joan Simpson, Simon Watt, John S. White, and Bear & Cara Williams. They've made valuable suggestions, corrections and comments regarding the portions of this book they examined. They are not responsible for any possible errors, nor do they necessarily endorse the material contained in this book.

Dreaming Down Under, Carrie Ginsberg Fine Gems, Elaine Ferrari, Hubert Inc., Nevada Mineral & Book Company, New Era Gems and Andrew Sarosi. Their stones or jewelry have been used for some of the photographs.

Charles Albert, Inc, Eve Alfillé, Juan José Virgen Alatorre, Mark Anderson, Anita's Beads, Auction Market Resource, Bear Essentials, Blue Moon Enterprise, Martha Borzoni, Canadian Institute of Gemmology, Isaias Casanova, Ear Charms, Inc., David Clay Company, Columbia Gem House, Dancing Designs, Division of Minerals and Energy Resources, South Australia, Jessica Dow, Coast-to-Coast Rarestones International, Erica Courtney, Paula Crevoshay, Tom DeGasperis, Barbara Eberle, Anthony de Goutière, Paul de Goutière, Devon Fine Jewelry, Different Seasons Jewelry, Mia Dixon, Jessica Dow, Robert Drummond, John and Lydia Dyer, Gemmological Association of All Japan (GAAJ) Zenhokyo Lab, David Greene, Gübelin Gem Lab, William Hanneman, Henry Hänni, Yossi Harari, Hubert Inc, Idaho Opal and Gem Corp, International School of Gemology, Michael Jakubowski, Robert James, Jewels by Woods, Rebecca Paquette-Johnson Richard Krementz Gemstones, Wolf Kuehn, Lang Antique & Estate Jewelry, Shoulin Lee, Gail Levine, Anna Malsy, Mayer & Watt, Wimon Manorotkul, Muse Imports, Nevada Mineral & Book Co, New Era Gems, Anatoly Novik, Omi Gems, Opalos de México, Pala International, Sami Fine Jewelry, Susan Sadler, Mark Schneider Design, Tony Seideman, Sherris Cottier Shank, Elise Skalwold, SSEF Swiss Gemological Institute, Gerald Stockton, Timeless Gems, TsavoriteOne, Larry Walker, Geoffrey Watt, Brad Weber, Emil Weis Opals, Jeff White, John S. White, Wilensky Fine Minerals, Bear Williams, Larry Woods, Wright's Rock Shop, Zaffiro, and Clay Zava. Photos and/or diagrams from them have been reproduced in this book.

Frank Chen and Joyce Ng. They provided technical assistance.

Louise Harris Berlin, editor of *Exotic Gems, Volume 2.* Thanks to her, this book is easier to read and understand.

My sincere thanks to all of these contributors for their kindness and help.

Exotic Gems

The term "exotic" has a variety of interpretations. The *Random House College Dictionary* defines it as "1. of foreign origin or character; 2. Striking or unusual in effect or appearance." Although people generally agree with these meanings, their minds conjure different images when "exotic" is used to describe something such as a gem. In order to discover connotations associated with "exotic," I asked six people from different backgrounds how they would define "exotic" and "exotic gems." Here are their responses, which I received via e-mail or in person:

1. *Unusual and exquisite; it can also have the connotation of burlesque, voluptuous or risqué. An exotic gem would be one like a diamond that is found deep in the interior of the earth, far from the surface.* A male American architect.

2. *For the French, "exotic" gives rise to dreams and refers to something coming from elsewhere, a foreign country, especially a tropical country: Island, sun, luxurious vegetation, heat, hibiscus flowers, One would never think of a Scandinavian country, for example, when you hear the word "exotic".* A Parisian woman whose hobby is traveling abroad on her own for months at a time.

3. *"Exotic" relates to the imagination of the reader and would mean, to the one who is home in the West, something slightly magic about places he or she might be dreaming of, if she/he has not been there. . . . I am not crazy about using this word for describing something that varies tremendously, such as a gem.* A French gem dealer who spends over half the year traveling throughout Asia.

4. *I have a Synonym Finder book which I use often. My answer before I looked it up was something unusual or way out. The book has many names for it. Here are a few, striking, fabulous, remarkable, out of the ordinary, extraordinary, marvelous, wondrous, unique, exciting, glamorous, sensational, thrilling, impressive.* A retired woman from Florida. Her husband, a retired fireman added. *HERE ARE A FEW I DON'T THINK YOU MEAN. HA HA: topless, bottomless, go-go, disco.*

5. *My interpretation is anything very unusual or out of the ordinary or eye 'catching' when you can't only say 'it's beautiful'. Personally my eyes focus on pearls only, without the diamonds.* A South African woman who has traveled extensively.

6. *In describing gemstones I would use "exotic-looking gem". The word exotic can mean gorgeous or alluring, and all these terms could be applied to a fine Kashmir sapphire or a parcel of Paraiba tourmalines or even a belly dancer. I've watched tropical sunsets that could be described as exotic.* A Canadian jeweler and gemologist.

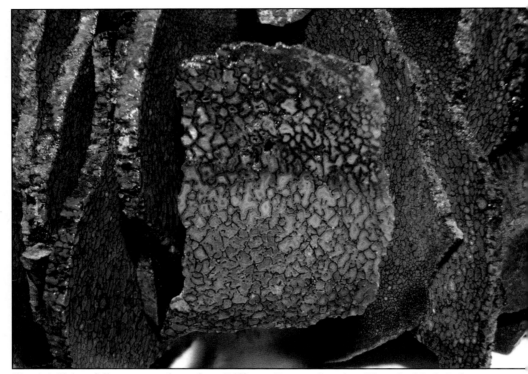

Fig. 1.1 Slabs of dinosaur gembone from Different Seasons Jewelry. *Photo by Mark Anderson.*

All of the gems featured in this book can be considered exotic even though they were not mentioned during my interviews. Kyanite, andalusite and sillimanite are so unusual that many people have never heard of them, nor are they aware that these three minerals have the same chemical composition. These gems are different because their crystal structure and the arrangement of their atoms are not the same. Despite their rarity, the gems can be found in jewelry as well as at gem shows.

Agatized dinosaur bone is strikingly different (fig 1.1). Though normally sold in rock and mineral shops, it is sometimes found in traditional jewelry stores. In fact, even agatized dinosaur dung is used in jewelry.

Garnet and common opal (opal with no play of color) may seem ordinary, but after you view the wide range of varieties and learn where they come from, I think you will agree they are not at all "common" and can be considered exotic. Fire opal (opal with a body color that is yellow, orange, red or brownish) is also discussed in this book. More than twenty novels have been written with "fire opal" in their title, but I haven't found any nonfiction books that focus on the identification and evaluation of fire opal or common opal. On the other hand, I own eight books with in-depth information on Australian black, boulder, white and matrix opal. Rather than rehash what has already been written about Australian opal, I've decided to concentrate on common and fire opal in this book. If you would like to see an eight-page-illustrated overview of all opals, consult my *Gemstone Buying Guide.*

Alexandrite and cat's-eye chrysoberyl are also featured in this volume. They easily qualify as exotic gems. Both are unusual, alluring and eye-catching, and most are now found in tropical countries such as Brazil, Sri Lanka, Tanzania, and India.

Much has been written about diamonds, rubies, sapphires, emeralds, and pearls, but most other gems are usually grouped together in general gem books with limited information on each stone. Since readers have requested additional information on the less common types, I decided to create a series of books entitled *Exotic Gems*, which explores each gem more in depth. The first volume covered tanzanite, rhodochrosite, zultanite, ammolite, and the feldspar group, which includes moonstone, sunstone, and labradorite. This volume features chrysoberyls, dinosaur gembone, andalusite, kyanite, sillimanite, common opal, fire opal and the garnet group.

This book includes comprehensive identification tables and tips on detecting

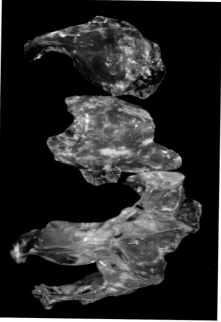

Fig. 1.2 Freeform fire opals and water opal from Mexico. *Opals courtesy Emil Weis Opals; photo by Tanja Schütz.*

imitations, lab-grown gems and gem treatments. I also discuss the history, geographic sources and metaphysical lore of the gems. Among the gems in this book, red garnet is probably the oldest and best-known gemstone. Primitive garnet jewelry dating as far back as 3000 BC has been found in Egypt. In biblical times, Noah was said to have used the garnet's red glow to guide his way through darkness while on the ark.

My gem guides typically contain more information on gemstone evaluation than those by other authors; this book is no exception. Evaluation guidelines and pricing ranges are given for each gem and close-up photos illustrate quality differences. If you learn how to judge gem quality, it will be easier for you to understand pricing and the uniqueness of the gems you buy. If you would like further information about gemstone evaluation and identification, you can find it in my *Gemstone Buying Guide, Diamond Handbook*, and *Volume 1* of *Exotic Gems*.

Before I wrote this book, I regarded kyanite as just a rock-hound type gemstone of little significance. After I learned more about it and saw examples of gem-grade material, I gained respect for kyanite and its potential beauty. Similarly, my appreciation for the other gems in this book has grown too. I hope that *Exotic Gems: Volume II* will awaken your interest in the multitude of intriguing gems that nature has to offer. If it does, I think you'll find that discovering new gems is a fascinating and worthwhile pursuit—and great fun, as well.

2

Chrysoberyl

lexandrite and chrysoberyl cat's-eye look very different, yet they are both
chrysoberyl, a mineral which may also be a transparent gem with a single color
(typically yellow, greenish yellow, green, or brown, or occasionally greenish blue).
The name originates from the Greek *chrysos,* meaning "golden" and alluding to the
frequent yellow color of the gem, its beryllium content and the mineral beryl. It
wasn't until 1789 that chrysoberyl was identified as a distinct species by German
geologist Abraham G. Werner.

In the 19th century, yellow chrysoberyl was in high demand for Victorian jewelry.
Brazilians called it "chrysolite," which means "golden stone" and they even named
a city after it. However, the term "crysolite" was confusing because it was also used
to refer to the gem peridot. During the 20th century, supplies of yellow chrysoberyl
dwindled, and it was overshadowed by alexandrite and cat's-eye chrysoberyl. New
finds have renewed interest in all chrysoberyl varieties. One of the most unusual is
cat's-eye alexandrite, which displays both chatoyancy and a color change.

Chapters 3 and 4 provide background information on cat's-eye chrysoberyl and
color-change chrysoberyl (alexandrite) as well as information on how they are
evaluated and priced. This chapter focuses on single-color chrysoberyl.

Geographic Sources of Chrysoberyl

The state of Minas Gerais in Brazil has been the most important source of all
chrysoberyl varieties. They are found in coarse-grained volcanic rock formations
called pegmatites, which are associated with quartz, garnet, tourmaline, yellow beryl,
aquamarine, topaz and other minerals. The variety alexandrite, on the other hand, is
found in schists. (Schists are metamorphic rocks formed under great pressure and
composed of minerals such as mica in parallel orientation.)

The second key source of all varieties of chrysoberyl is Sri Lanka. Besides having
perhaps the oldest chrysoberyl deposits, Sri Lanka is noted for its high quality cat's-
eye chrysoberyl and alexandrite.

In 1996, green and bluish-green chrysoberyl appeared at the Tucson Gem Show,
It was reportedly from Tanzania and the lighter material was marketed as "mint"
chrysoberyl (Gems & Gemology Fall 1996 P 215). The green color was caused by
the presence of the mineral element vanadium. Consequently, this new color of
chrysoberyl was called vanadium chrysoberyl. A few stones had a highly saturated
green color and they were difficult to distinguish from lab-grown single-color green
chrysoberyl (*Gems & Gemology* Summer 2003, p 144). Vanadium chrysoberyl,
which has also been found in Sri Lanka (fig 2.3), is extremely rare.

Another relatively new find of chrysoberyl is Orissa, India. Yellow and greenish
yellow chrysoberyl has been available from there since around 2001. Other commercial sources of chrysoberyl include Madagascar. Burma and Zimbabwe.

Fig. 2.1 Faceted and rough chrysoberyl. © *H. A. Hänni, SSEF Swiss Gemmological Institute.*

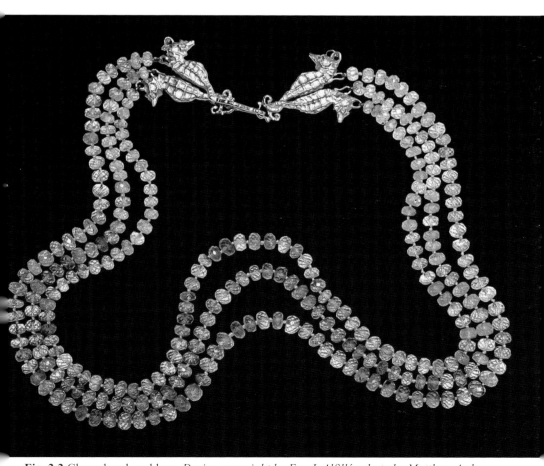

Fig. 2.2 Chrysoberyl necklace. *Design copyright by Eve J. Alfillé; photo by Matthew Arden.*

Fig. 2.3 Vanadium chrysoberyl from Sri Lanka. *Necklace by Zaffiro; chrysoberyl from Mayer & Watt; photo by Daniel Van Rossen.*

Fig. 2.4 Sri Lankan chrysoberyl (4.60 cts.). *Necklace from de Goutière Jewellers; photo by Paul de Goutière.*

Fig. 2.5 Chrysoberyl (54.59 cts) from Mayer & Watt. *Photo: Geoffrey D. Watt.*

Fig. 2.6 Chrysoberyl cut by J. L. White Fine Gemstones. *Photo by Jeff White.*

Fig. 2.7 Chrysoberyl (2.08 cts) cut by John Dyer. *Photo by Lydia Dyer.*

Fig. 2.8 Chrysoberyl by J. L. White Fine Gemstones. *Photo: Jeff White.*

Metaphysical Properties of Chrysoberyl

According to some crystal enthusiasts, chrysoberyl can help you manifest monetary wealth, job promotions, and business success while at the same time allowing you to release your attachment to material goods so that your life is not governed by them. In addition, chrysoberyl brings peace of mind and promotes understanding of interpersonal relationships. Using chrysoberyl concurrently with other stones that emit healing energy for specific medical problems enhances their energy transmittal. It is also said that chrysoberyl:

♦ Increases spiritual and personal power
♦ Allows you to see the good in your surroundings
♦ Brings compassion and forgiveness
♦ Regulates the secretion of adrenalin
♦ Moderates cholesterol levels
♦ Cleanses and balances the liver, kidneys and gall bladder

Identifying Characteristics of Chrysoberyl

Chrysoberyl is an ideal stone for men's rings and everyday wear because of its durability and stability to light, heat and chemicals. No other natural gemstone except ruby, sapphire and diamond is harder than chrysoberyl (8.5 on the Mohs hardness scale). Its brilliance, rarity and unique varieties make it a desirable gem worth imitating and creating in laboratories.

Transparent chrysoberyl with no color change can be confused with natural and synthetic sapphire, peridot, tourmaline, citrine, garnet, natural and synthetic spinel, and other green and yellow stones. The key properties that will distinguish chrysoberyl from other gems are refractive index (RI), pleochroism, birefringence, optic figure, and spectrum, whose values are indicated in the table below. However, these will not separate natural from synthetic chrysoberyl.

Magnification is required for separating natural from lab-grown chrysoberyl. Man-made flame-fusion or melt process stones may contain bubbles or curved straie and some needle-like inclusions. Natural chrysoberyls may also have needle inclusions, but they can also contain distinctive crystals, steplike formations called twinning planes, and cavities filled with a liquid and a bubble of gas, which are called two-phase inclusions. Major gem labs also use high tech equipment to help determine the chemistry of the gems. Information on synthetic alexandrite is provided in Chapter 4.

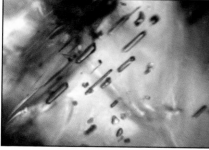

Fig. 2.9 Chrysoberyl inclusions. *Photo by Anthony de Goutière.*

Fig. 2.10 Crystal inclusions in chrysoberyl. *Photo by Anthony de Goutière.*

Identifying Characteristics of Chrysoberyl

RI: 1.74–1.76	SG: 3.64–3.80	Birefringence: 0.008–0.012
Dispersion: 0.005 Hardness:	Hardness: 8.5	Polish luster: Vitreous to subadamatine
Toughness: Good–excellent	Crystal System: Orthorhombic Optic Char: DR, biaxial +	
Fracture: Conchoidal with a vitreous to greasy luster	Cleavage: Distinct 1 direction, seldom observed, varies to poor. (Joel Arem)	

Pleochroism: Weak to moderate trichroism in transparent yellow, green and brown varieties, usually different tones of the bodycolor. Strong green, orange and purple trichroism in alexandrite. In cat's-eye, the lower the transparency, the harder it is to see the pleochroism, which is in light to medium tones of the bodycolor.

Spectrum: A diagnostic band centered at 444–445 nm in the blue/violet characterizes most yellow to green and brown chrysoberyls including cat's-eyes, which are typically colored by iron. When the stone has a strong color, two additional lines can be seen at 505 and 485 nm in the green-blue. The GIA *Gem Identification Lab Manual* (p. 198) states that intense bluish green stones might also show additional bands and lines with a band between 590 nm and 665 nm and an emission line at 670 nm.

The typical alexandrite spectrum varies with pleochroism. According to the GIA *Gem Identification Lab Manual* (p. 196), in the purple-red direction, there are strong lines in the red at 678 nm and 680.5 nm; weaker ones 645 nm and 655 nm; a broad absorption between about 540 nm and 605 nm; weak lines in the blue at 468 nm, 473 nm, and 476.5 nm; and a cutoff in the violet. In the green pleochroic direction, there are strong lines in the red at 678 nm and 680.5 nm; weaker ones at 645 nm, 649 nm 655 nm, and 665 nm; a broad absorption between about 555 nm and 640 nm and a cutoff in the violet at about 470 nm. In the orange pleochroic direction, there are no strong absorptions. The spectrum of synthetic alexandrite is the same as that of natural alexandrite.

Fluorescence: Yellow and greenish yellow—inert to yellowish green (SW); other colors usually inert; cat's-eye—inert; alexandrite & cat's-eye alexandrite—inert to moderate red (LW and SW)

Crystal habit (form): Tabular crystals, often twinned and striated. Broken fragments are common and the crystals are found as waterworn pebbles in gravel.

Geological setting: Occurs in pegmatites, mica schists, and as stream pebbles.

Stability: Stable to heat and light; no reaction to chemicals. The British Gemmological Association (Gem A) advises avoiding the jewelers' torch with cat's-eyes.

Treatments: Normally none. Occasionally fractures may be masked with fillers. John Koivula reports in *Photoatlas of Inclusions, Volume 2* (p 372) that neutron irradiation has been used to change light brownish yellow cat's-eyes into a deep slightly reddish brown, which in some instances is almost black.

Most of the technical data in the above table was based on *Gems: Fourth Edition* by Robert Webster, *Color Encyclopedia of Gemstones (1987)* by Joel Arem, www.mindat.org, *GIA Gem Reference Guide,* the GIA *Gem Identification Lab Manual* (2005), the Gem A *Diploma in Gemmology Course* (2009), *Identification of Gemstones* by Michael O'Donoghue & Louise Joyner, *Photoatlas of Inclusions, Vol 2* by John Koivula. and *Gems & Gemology*, Spring 1988, pp 16-32.

Fig. 2.11 Chrysoberyl cut by John Dyer. *Photo by Lydia Dyer.*

Fig. 2.12 Chrysoberyl ring design copyright by Eve J. Alfillé. *Photo: Matthew Arden.*

Evaluation of Single-Color Chrysoberyl & Pricing Ranges

Generally, the stronger the color, the higher the price. Stones that approach an emerald green color are rare and are the highest priced, a few thousand dollars per carat, but they are difficult if not impossible to find. Yellow to yellowish green stones have similar values and retail for less than $800 per carat. Many chrysoberyls have a brownish green to yellow color, particularly those from Sri Lanka. Their brown secondary color prevents them from being classified as fine color and consequently, they sell for much less. Nevertheless, when such stones are well-cut they can be very attractive in jewelry. Some material from Tanzania has a rare bright yellow-green color. It is prized and sells at premium prices if you can find it.

Clarity and transparency are important price factors, too. Fine-cut stones fetch higher prices than stones with windowing (fig. 2.13) because stones without windows are more attractive, and more weight is lost from the rough when cutting them.

Fig. 2.13 Windowing (see-through effect). Large, small and medium windows. *Photo © R. Newman.*

Yellow to yellowish-green chrysoberyls from 1–3 carats in size range from about $20–$200 per carat retail. Stones 5-carat and above can retail for around $50–$800 per carat. Chrysoberyls above 15 carats are not common, yet they do not increase in per-carat price with size. Larger chrysoberyls, in fact, are often cheaper in per-carat price than smaller stones because it is easier to sell stones under ten carats. The largest cut chrysoberyl may be a 114-carat cushion-cut at the Smithsonian Institution.

Caring for Chrysoberyl

Clean chrysoberyl with warm water, soap and a soft brush. Ultrasonics and steamers are safe if the stone has a good clarity. Of all the gems in this book, chrysoberyl is the most resistant to scratching and chipping. Overall, chrysoberyl is a durable gemstone well suited for everyday wear in rings and other jewelry.

3

Cat's-eye Chrysoberyl

Many gems can reflect a band of light if they are cut as a cabochon (with a smooth domed shape) and have parallel fiberlike or hollow tube inclusions. This phenomenon makes them resemble the eyes of a cat. As a result, the gem trade calls them cat's-eyes. This book shows examples of chrysoberyl, opal, garnet, andalusite and sillimanite stones with a cat's-eye appearance. However, when the term cat's-eye is used alone, it refers to chrysoberyl. Other cat's-eyes are generally prefaced or followed by the name of the stone, for example, cat's-eye opal or opal cat's-eye. There are several spellings of cat's-eye (catseye, cat's eye, cats-eye, etc.). All seem to be correct. I use cat's-eye—the same form as that of the Gemological Institute of America (GIA) and the British Gemmological Association (Gem A).

The gemological term for the cat's-eye effect is **chatoyancy**, which derives from the French *chatoyer* meaning "to gleam like a cat's eyes." If a chrysoberyl contains enough fiber-like inclusions (called silk), it's a candidate for cutting as a cat's-eye gem. In chrysoberyl, the silk is often so fine that a microscope is needed to see the fibers (fig. 3.1) and even when magnified, they may be hard to see. That's why the "eye" in chrysoberyl is the sharpest of any gem with a cat's-eye effect. In rare cases, the inclusions create a 4-ray star instead of a single band.

Not all cat's-eye gems contain fibers. John S. White, former curator of gems and minerals at the Smithsonian Institution, says that "the best tourmaline cat's-eye in the Smithsonian collection contains no fibers at all, it is perfectly clean. The effect in this case comes from parallel striations from an original crystal face left untouched on the flat bottom of the stone. In fact, any cutter could create excellent cat's-eyes in a clean stone by inscribing fine rulings on the bottom of the cab."

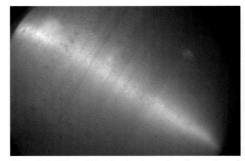

Fig. 3.1 Fiber-like inclusions in chrysoberyl cat's-eye that cause the eye. *Photomicrograph by Anthony de Goutière.*

Cat's-eye has the longest history of any of the chrysoberyl varieties. Though known in Asia as far back as the first century, it didn't become popular in Europe until the late 19th century when the English Duke of Connaught gave a cat's-eye engagement ring to Princess Louise Margaret of Prussia. This sparked a huge increase in the price of chrysoberyl cat's-eye. Today, it is especially prized in Hong Kong and Japan.

In his book *Gemstones: Quality and Value, Volume 2*, dealer Yasakuwa Suwa says that "although cat's-eye is a gemstone favored by men in the United States, relatively small cat's-eyes weighing two to three carats are often fashioned and sold as women's rings in the Japanese market."

Fig. 3.2 Cat's-eye ring and photo from Richard Krementz Gemstones.

Fig. 3.3 Cat's-eye ring from *Lang Antique & Estate Jewelry. Photo by Thomas Picarella.*

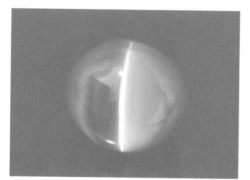

Fig. 3.4 Cat's-eye (13.25 cts) from Pala Gems International. *Photo by Jason Stephenson.*

Fig. 3.5 Same cat's-eye showing an open eye. *From Pala Gems. Photo: Jason Stephenson.*

Geographic Sources of Cat's-eye Chrysoberyl

Sri Lanka is home to the most prestigious and probably the oldest cat's-eye deposits. The stones are collected in pit mines among gem gravels. Brazil and India are also key sources. In addition, cat's-eye is found in Myanmar, Zimbabwe, Madagascar and Tanzania.

Metaphysical Properties of Cat's-eye

Cat's-eye is believed to be a magical stone that brings happiness, serenity and good luck. People with eye disorders are advised to wear cat's-eye because it is said to improve eye problems and night vision. Cat's-eye is also used to relieve headaches and facial pain. An excellent meditative tool, cat's-eye is said to facilitate remote viewing, perception of other dimensions, communication with angels, and a rediscovery of one's life.

Fig. 3.6 Tiger's-eye quartz. *Photo © R. Newman.*   **Fig. 3.7** Cat's-eye tourmaline. © Newman.

Other Stones that Resemble Cat's-eye Chrysoberyl

The most common cat's-eye lookalikes are:

- quartz cat's-eye
- actinolite cat's-eye
- apatite cat's-eye
- bleached tiger's-eye quartz
- tourmaline cat's-eye
- cat's-eye glass

The key features used in distinguishing chrysoberyl cat's-eye from imitations are refractive index (1.75 spot reading is typical), spectrum (a strong band at 444 nm), and specific gravity (3.73 +/-0.02).

Evaluation of Cat's-eye Chrysoberyl & Pricing Ranges

The quality of the "eye" is a major value factor for cat's-eye chrysoberyl, but color, clarity, transparency, and cut also play a role in determining price. These are discussed separately below:

"Eye" (chatoyancy)

Top stones display the following characteristics:

- **A distinct sharp eye**. It shouldn't be too wide, nor thread-thin, and it should stand out from the background with good contrast. Ideally, the band of reflected light is white or gray, not the same color hue as the stone's background.

- **An eye that extends all the way across the stone**. The line of the eye should not be interrupted with inclusions or be a partial line.

- **A well-centered eye**. The eye should be in the center of the stone and run lengthwise, not diagonally or to the side of the stone.

- **A straight band of light**. If the stone is not smooth and well cut, the band may appear wavy. Straight bands are generally preferred.

- **A good opening and closing of the eye**. This occurs when the cat's-eye is held between two lights and rotated. The band splits into two bands that move apart and then merge again as if the stone is winking at you. (figs. 3.4, 3.5, 3.8 & 3.9).

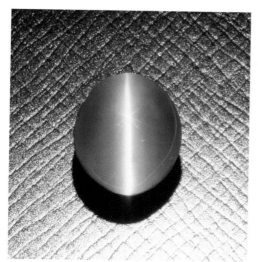

Fig. 3.8 Chrysoberyl cat's-eye from the Andrew Sarosi Collection. *Photo © Renée Newman.*

Fig. 3.9 Same cat's-eye with an open eye. *Photo © Renée Newman.*

♦ **A "milk and honey" effect.** This results when the stone is illuminated from the side by a beam of light. The half of the stone nearest the light shows the body color of the stone, while the other half looks milky. When the gemstone is rotated, the colors switch (fig. 3.10).

Color

Natural-color cat's-eye generally ranges from brown to yellow to yellowish or grayish green. Irradiated cat's-eyes, which are rare, may also be black or gray. The color of most chrysoberyls is natural and not the result of treatment.

Fig. 3.10 Same cat's-eye with a "milk and honey" effect. *Photo © Renée Newman.*

Simon Watt of Mayer & Watt describes the ideal color of chrysoberyl cat's-eye as a golden, yellowy, slightly greenish honey color without being brown and without any of the colors taking precedence. The GIA *Colored Stones* course (2002) describes the most prized body color as a golden yellow, slightly greenish or brownish yellow "honey" color with a silvery eye whose "milk and honey" appearance is slightly brownish yellow on one side and yellowish green on the other. Indian cat's-eyes tend to be more green and not the classic honey color, but they have been selling well. Keep in mind that color is a matter of personal choice and that any cat's-eye may be attractive if it has a distinct eye and acceptable clarity.

Clarity

Chrysoberyl cat's-eyes are filled with many parallel fiber-like inclusions, which create the band of light. Fractures, cavities, and crystals that interrupt the band of light or detract from the color of the stone are considered undesirable. However, if the lowered clarity is not too distracting, it may allow you to buy a decent stone for a much lower price than normal. Chrysoberyl is noted for its durability and resistance to scratching, but if you're buying the stone for an everyday ring, avoid one with eye-visible cracks.

Transparency

Cat's-eyes must be at least slightly cloudy in order to display a distinct eye. Top stones, however, will have good translucency, meaning that light can readily pass through them. In other words, the highest priced cat's-eyes are milky but not too milky, and definitely not semi-opaque. When checking for translucency and clarity, shine a penlight into the stone from the bottom to see if inclusions block the passage of light. Heavily included stones should be discounted.

Fig. 3.11 Sri Lankan cat's-eye (72 cts) pendant from Bear Essentials. *Photo by Bear Williams.*

Cut quality

If cat's-eyes have a distinct, centered straight band, they are probably well cut. However if they have high domes, they may be discounted because they will look small for their weight, the eye will appear to be trapped at the top of the stone, and they may be impractical for jewelry. Flat stones will have a good spread and look larger than their actual weight, but the eye will most likely be wide and not well defined. Consequently, well-proportioned stones with medium domes are the most in demand. The shape should also be pleasing to the eye.

Price ranges of chrysoberyl cat's-eyes

Low-grade cat's-eyes below a carat in weight sell for as little as $20 a carat. Expect to pay at least $200 per carat for good quality and $500 or more for high quality. Commercial quality cat's-eyes from one to two carats retail for about $150–$600 per carat, whereas top quality stones may sell for as much as $3000 per carat. In sizes above two carats, high quality stones retail from $2000– $7000 per carat, In sizes above 10 carats, the weight may decrease the per-carat price of the stone because such stones are more difficult to sell.

If you're looking for the "perfect" cat's-eye, you probably won't find it. Chrysoberyl cat's-eyes are rare. If you'd like to enjoy their exotic beauty, be prepared to compromise on either color, clarity, cut or the quality of the eye.

4

Alexandrite

The wonderful alexandrite is an emerald by day and an amethyst at night. Edwin Streeter, *Precious Stones and Gems* (1898).

Alexandrite was discovered in the early 1830's in the emerald mines of Russia's Ural Mountains near the Tokovaya River. The name alexandrite was officially accepted in 1842 in honor of Tzar Alexander II. Since the stone only occurred in Russia and its red and green colors mirrored those of the Imperial Russian flag, it became the national stone of tsarist Russia. Some people have said that alexandrite's green color in daylight represented the hope Alexander II brought to Russia when he emancipated the serfs and initiated the transformation of the agrarian Russian economy into an industrial state. The red by candlelight prophesied the bloody revolution that brought an end to the tsarist regime *(Alexandrite Tsarstone Collector's Guide,* Chapter 1, www.alexandrite.net).

By the late 1800's, Russian alexandrite was not only prized by jewelers in St. Petersburg and Paris, it was also a favorite stone of Tiffany's, which was responsible for popularizing it in America. As the Russian deposits became exhausted, interest in the gem waned. Today, Russian alexandrite is found primarily in estate jewelry and museums. However, new discoveries in the late 1900's, particularly in Brazil, have revived interest in the stone. It helps that alexandrite is the alternate birthstone for June and the 55th wedding anniversary stone.

Alexandrite is the most famous and expensive chrysoberyl variety. It is defined by its color change which ranges from purple red or lavender in incandescent light (e.g., light bulb, halogen light, candlelight) to bluish green or greenish blue in daylight or fluorescent light. Few gems show as complete of a color change as alexandrite, and consequently the phenomenon itself is called the **alexandrite effect**. Trace amounts of chromium and vanadium account for this shift in color, along with traces of iron. Alexandrite can also show the cat's-eye effect if it has enough fiber-like inclusions (front cover, 4.13, & 4.14).

Fig. 4.1 Alexandrite in daylight (left) and incandescent light (right). *Rings by Hubert Inc; photo by Diamond Graphics.*

Because of alexandrite's prestige, ordinary chrysoberyl is occasionally sold as alexandrite. At a gem show, a seller showed me two yellowish green chrysoberyls with a lab certificate stating they were alexandrites. They didn't change color and I had never heard of the lab that issued the reports. If a chrysoberyl doesn't change color when moved from daylight to incandescent light, it is not an alexandrite.

Fig. 4.2 Brazilian alexandrite (3.03 cts) (daylight) from Mayer & Watt. *Photo Geoffrey Watt.*

Fig. 4.3 Same alexandrite (incandescent). *Mayer & Watt; photo by Geoffrey D. Watt.*

Left: Fig. 4.4 Alexandrite (18.50 cts) from Sri Lanka. The hammer price for the Edwardian platinum brooch was $125,000 at a Phillips de Pury & Company (New York) auction on May 15, 2001. *Photo from Gail Brett Levine's www.Auction Market Resource.com.*

Geographic Sources of Alexandrite

Between the 1830's and 1900 Russia was the main source of alexandrite. No significant amount of new material has been reported there

Fig. 4.5 Tanzanian alexandrite rough and photo from New Era Gems.

since the Russian revolution in 1917. In 1987, high-quality alexandrite was found in Brazil, at Hematita, Minas Gerais. The Hematita mine is still important, but other sources include Tanzania, Sri Lanka, Zimbabwe, Madagascar, and the Brazilian state of Bahia. In 1993, alexandrite was also discovered in the states of Orissa and Madhya Pradesh, India. Since then, India has become a significant source of faceted and cat's-eye alexandrite.

Identification of Alexandrite

Distinguishing alexandrite from other natural gems is relatively easy because of its unique color change and trichroism (greenish, orange-yellow and purple-red). Its refractive index (1.74–1.76) and other gemological properties are provided in the chrysoberyl identification table in Chapter 2.

Since there's a good market for stones that resemble alexandrite, man-made look-alikes have been created. Synthetic (lab-grown) alexandrite is the most difficult to separate from natural alexandrite because both have basically the same chemical composition and most of their physical and optical properties are the same. However, strong red fluorescence indicates the stone is synthetic. The fluorescence of natural alexandrite only ranges from none to moderate red.

Magnification is the key test for determining if a stone is natural or not. Figures 4.6–4.9 show examples of natural alexandrite inclusions, which not only help determine if the stones were mined but also where they were mined. Natural stones can have angular crystals, negative crystals, liquid inclusions, needle-like inclusions, "fingerprints," and twinning. For more information on the identification of alexandrite and their geographic sources with magnification as well as with high tech equipment, see *Russian Alexandrites* by Karl Schmetzer (Published by Schweizerbart Science Publishers, Stuttgart, September 2010). Anna-Kathrin Malsy, one of the contributors to the book, provided the examples below.

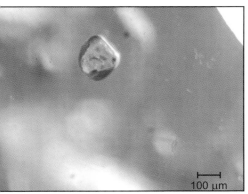

Fig. 4.6 Octahedral fluorite crystal in an alexandrite from Hematita, Brazil. This inclusion has so far only been recognized in gems from Hematita. *Anna Malsy / Gübelin Gem Lab.*

Fig. 4.7 Slightly rounded zircon crystal with conspicuous stress cracks and accompanied by a line of tiny light scattering particles. Zircon inclusions are frequently encountered in Sri Lankan alexandrites. *Anna Malsy / Gübelin Gem Lab.*

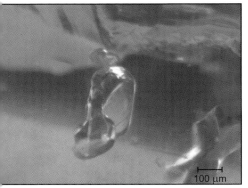

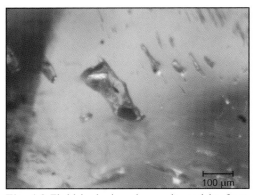

Fig. 4.8 Well-developed, euhedral apatite crystal with a smaller crystal attached on the side in an alexandrite from Lake Manyara, Tanzania. *Anna Malsy / Gübelin Gem Lab.*

Fig. 4.9 Fluid inclusions in an alexandrite from the Ural Mountains, Russia. *Anna Malsy / the Gübelin Gem Lab.*

Even though lab-grown alexandrite is found in jewelry, it is primarily used for lasers. Alexandrite lasers were originally developed for government and military applications by AlliedSignal Corp. Other companies synthesize the stone, too. The Northrop Grumman Space Technology website states that alexandrite is one of the most robust solid-state laser materials available and that its unique combination of properties offer application in such areas as dermatology, spectroscopy, testing of fiber optics and photodetectors, pumping of dye lasers, nonlinear optics studies and annealing of semiconductors. Northrup Grumman's synthetic alexandrite is named **allexite,** which should not be confused with **alexite**, a glass imitation of alexandrite.

Fig. 4.10 Chatham Created Alexandrite ring and photo by Tom DeGasperis.

In *Identification of Gemstones* (p 141*)*, Michael O'Donoghue and Louise Joyner discuss other companies that have synthesized alexandrite. Creative Crystals Inc. of San Ramon California reported growing it in 1973. The Japanese firms Seiko and Kyocera have also made alexandrite, marketed in the U.S. as Inamori Created Alexandrite. In 1987, Kyocera was the first to produce a commercially available synthetic cat's-eye alexandrite.

Since the early 1980's, lab-grown alexandrite has been produced at various locations in the former USSR. For more information on Russian synthetic alexandrite, see the Fall 1996 issue of *Gems & Gemology* (pp 186-202).

The GIA Gem Identification Lab Manual (2005, p 197) lists the inclusions characteristic of the three types of synthetic alexandrite growth methods:

Flux: Hexagonal or triangular metallic platelets, tubes or parallel planes of flux, uniform straight or angular growth lines and veil-like inclusions

Pulled: Needle-like inclusions, curved striae, tiny gas bubbles

Floating zone: Gas bubbles, swirled appearance

The most common substitutes for natural alexandrite are color-change synthetic sapphire (sometimes called **alexandrine**) and synthetic spinel. Alexandrite may also be confused with andalusite and color-change garnet, which is occasionally sold as alexandrite garnet. **Zandrite** is a glass that imitates alexandrite. It is available in two colors: pink and purple. Zandrite that is pink in incandescent light turns green under fluorescent lighting, whereas purple zandrite turns blue. The change of color is caused by the presence of the mineral neodymium. These imitations can be separated from natural alexandrite by their refractive index, pleochroism, spectrum, and specific gravity. Size and clarity can be good clues for lay people. If a color-change stone is large and eye-clean, it most likely is not natural alexandrite. Alexandrites above five carats are rare, and even smaller stones usually have eye-visible inclusions. Likewise, beware of unusually low prices, which suggest that the stones may be imitations.

Fig. 4.11 Alexandrites (daylight). *Ring by Omi Gems; photo by Diamond Graphics.*

Fig. 4.12 Alexandrites (incandescent light). *Ring by Omi Gems; photo by Diamond Graphics.*

Metaphysical Properties of Alexandrite

Alexandrite is said to be a stone of joy, which allows the wearer to be as adaptable to different situations as the gem is to changing light sources. It is ideal for those who are daring, adventurous, and creative. Metaphysical specialists use alexandrite as a teaching stone on the spiritual level. When their students hold the stone in the palm or wear it on their forefinger or at their throat, they feel an openness of mind and heart that enables them to receive new information. The presence of the stone helps them raise their level of integrity in interactions with others.

The following benefits have been ascribed to alexandrite:

♦ Rebuilds self-respect
♦ Augments the power of love spells
♦ Repels undesirable people and energies
♦ Enhances color therapy
♦ Strengthens willpower
♦ Allows you to see both sides of an issue.
♦ Assists in balancing brain function
♦ Stimulates the pituitary gland.
♦ Heals disorders of the pancreas and spleen
♦ Helps you relax, which supports the healing process

Evaluation of Alexandrite & Pricing Ranges

The following factors affect the price of alexandrites:

Color change quality: The strength of the color change is the most important criterion for evaluating alexandrite. If there is no change from daylight to incandescent light, the stone is simply a chrysoberyl. The more dramatic and complete the change, the more valuable the alexandrite. Stones with a classification of 100% show a complete color change in all directions and on all the facets.

Fig. 4.13 Cat's-eye alexandrite from Pala Gems International. *Photo by Mia Dixon.*

Fig. 4.14 Cat's-eye alexandrite from Pala Gems International. *Photo by Mia Dixon.*

If half of the facets change color, the gem is classified as a 50% and so on. Most high-quality alexandrite is between 85–95%. The American Gemological Laboratories (AGL) rates the degree of color change on a seven step scale from faint to moderate, strong and prominent including transition degrees such as moderate to strong.

Color: The colors of the change are also important. A bluish green daylight color is more valued than yellowish green or brownish green. A purple-red or purple color in incandescent light is more coveted than a brownish color. Don't expect to see a color change from ruby red to emerald green. The "red" of alexandrite is typically more like an amethyst and the "green" is not as green and intense as in top-grade emeralds, but more like a tourmaline. The depth of color also plays a role in the price. Stones with medium to medium-dark tones are most valued, because they are pretty but still exhibit a strong color change. Light and very light tones are the least valued. Often stones with the most intense color change are just too dark in daylight. In addition, the less brown or gray that masks the color, the higher the price.

Be aware that lighting varies in color temperature, so some fluorescent bulbs can produce a stronger change and slightly different colors than others. Even in natural daylight, the color can vary depending on the time of day and condition of the sky. The optimal light conditions for the green color is daylight, but not direct sunlight; for the red, candlelight is best. Whenever possible, look at stones under a variety of lighting conditions before buying them.

Clarity and transparency: The clarity range of alexandrite is similar to that of ruby. It's difficult to find eye-clean stones above one carat and extremely difficult in sizes above three carats. Because of the numerous inclusions, the transparency is normally lower than that of gems such as amethyst. Semi-opaque stones are not considered gem quality and may sell for less than $20 per carat. The higher the clarity and better the transparency, the higher the price. However, if the alexandrite can be cut as an attractive cat's-eye as a result of the inclusions, it can fetch a good price. Nevertheless, it would sell for less than if it were transparent.

Cut quality: Because of the scarcity and high cost of the rough, alexandrites are generally cut to maximize the weight and color change instead of the brilliance. Consequently the cut quality is typically lower than that of ordinary chrysoberyl.

Fig. 4.15 Alexandrites (daylight). *Ring by Omi Gems; photo by Diamond Graphics.*

Fig. 4.16 Alexandrites (incandescent light). *Ring by Omi Gems; photo by Diamond Graphics.*

That being said, the better the proportioning and faceting of a gem, the greater the beauty and price and the easier it is to sell. If the stone has chatoyancy as well as color change, the cutter usually makes a careful compromise to achieve a pleasing cabochon that will exhibit both phenomena. Some color may have to be sacrificed to create a pleasing eye.

Carat weight: Alexandrites above five carats are extremely rare and usually of low quality. Fine quality alexandrites are expensive no matter how large or small they are. Even in sizes under one-half carat, they can sell for a few thousaand dollars per carat.

Geographic origin: For the most part, quality takes precedence over geographic origin. One exception is Russian alexandrites with respected lab documents. Because of their rarity, historical prestige and unique color change, they can sell for double the price of similar quality stones from other localities. It's comparable to the situation with Kashmir sapphires, which are also historically prestigious and now found mainly in estate jewelry. A few buyers may prefer stones from Brazil or Sri Lanka because of an emotional attachment or their history, but normally pricing is based on the quality of the alexandrite and not its source.

Pricing ranges of alexandrite: Between 2009 and 2010 prices of alexandrites increased as much as 50% because of a lower supply of rough from Brazil. In 2010, 1–3 carat alexandrites were retailing for up to $15,000 per carat. High quality 3-5 carat stones were retailing between $13,000–$30,000 per carat. As mentioned previously, stones below one-half carat are expensive, retailing for as much as $6,000 per carat in fine qualities. Alexandrite is a regal stone that fetches regal prices.

5

Agatized Dinosaur Bone & Poop

Look at figures 5.1 and 5.2. These images show a cross section of a human vertebra. Notice all the holes in the bone. These were passageways for blood vessels and bone marrow. The holes are called **cells** by dinobone dealers.

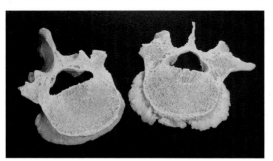

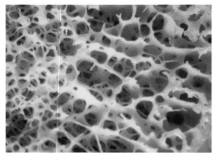

Fig. 5.1 Cross section of human vertebra. *Photo © Renée Newman.*

Fig. 5.2 Same vertebra magnified ten times. *Photo © Renée Newman.*

Fig. 5.3 shows a cross section of a dinosaur vertebra whose empty cells and spaces were partially replaced with minerals. In this example, most of the mineral material is **chalcedony,** an aggregate of microscopic quartz crystals, which is traditionally defined as cryptocrystalline quartz in America and polycrystalline quartz in Great Britain. Translucent chalcedony with patterns or bands is called **agate**, and dinosaur bones that have been replaced with agate are called **agatized dinosaur bone** or simply **dino bone** or **gembone. Opalized bone** is bone whose cells contain

Fig. 5.3 Partially mineralized dino bone from Different Seasons Jewelry. *Photo: Mark Anderson.*

common opal. Other minerals such as calcite and iron pyrite may also be found. Chalcedony, however, is the most frequent mineral found in gembone, which is why it is also called agatized dino bone even if other minerals are also present.

Dino bone that is sold legally has been found on private land in countries that permit its sale. It may be sold in rough form, as polished pieces or set in jewelry. Designers like gembone because it allows them to create distinctive one-of-a-kind jewelry pieces. Examples are shown in figures 5.4–5.8.

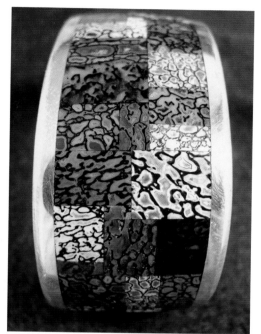

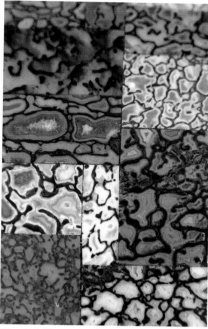

Fig. 5.4 Dinosaur gembone inlay cuff bracelet and photo by *Larry Walker.*

Fig. 5.5 Close-up view of gembone in fig. 5.4. *Bracelet and photo by Larry Walker.*

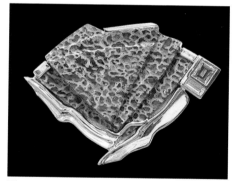

Fig. 5.6 Dinosaur gembone ring © Susan Sadler. *Photo from Susan Sadler.*

Fig. 5.7 Gembone pin design copyright by Eve J. Alfillé. *Photo by Matthew Arden.*

Fig. 5.8 Gembone rings from Different Seasons Jewelry. *Photo by David Greene.*

Basic Identification Data of Material in Dinobone Cells

While chalcedony is the most common gem material found in dinosaur bone, common opal, calcite, and pyrite can also be components. Their chemical composition, refractive index, density and hardness are provided below:

Agate (chalcedony):
Chemical composition: SiO_2 — silica (microcrystalline quartz)
RI: 1.53–1.54, SG: 2.58–2.64, Hardness: 6.5–7

Calcite:
Chemical composition: $CaCo_3$ — calcium carbonate
RI: 1.486–1.658, SG: 2.65–2.75, Hardness: 3

Opal:
Chemical composition: $SiO_2 \cdot H_2O$, — silica + water 3–10%
RI: 1.45 (+0.20, -0.80), SG: 2.15 (+.08, -.9), Hardness: 5–6.5

Pyrite:
Chemical composition: FeS_2 — Iron sulfide
RI: not determined because it is opaque, SG: 4.9–5.1, Hardness: 6–6.5

Coprolite (Fossilized Animal Excrement)

Coprolite, is the scientific name for fossilized animal droppings. It takes at least 10,000 years for organic material to fossilize. Older material has had more time to agatize. Coprolite is important to paleontologists because analysis of it can help them determine the food that ancient animals ate and the way they digested it. The term is derived from the Greek *kopro* (dung) and *lithos* (stone) and was coined in1829 by Dr. William Buckland, an English geologist and paleontologist.

Coprolite from Utah and Colorado may be agatized and have attractive patterns showing remnants of what dinosaurs ate. The size and color of these agate pockets are the most important determinants of coprolite's value unless there are large and unmistakable remains of bone or plant matter. These inclusions will increase the price of the stone.

Figure 5.11 shows an example of a rough specimen and a coprolite that was cut and polished to make a belt buckle. It is from Utah. Coprolite from other areas may only be a hardened fossil without gem material. Nevertheless, non-gem coprolite is sometimes used for beads, pendants and carvings. Needless to say, any coprolite can be an interesting conversation piece.

Where are Gembone and Coprolite Found?

The largest deposits of gembone are found in Utah and Colorado in the Morrison Formation, a late Jurassic series of sedimentary rock in the western United States and Canada, which consists of mudstone, sandstone, siltstone and limestone.

Figs 5.9 & 5.10 Left: Coprolite cuff links. Right: Coprolite ring. *Jewelry by Mark Anderson of Different Seasons Jewelry; photos by Jessica Dow.*

Fig. 5.11 Coprolite belt buckle & rough from Nevada Mineral & Book Co. *Photo © Newman.*

Fig. 5.12 Fossil reptile dung—Coprolite from Lewis County, Washington. *Coprolite & photo from Anita's Beads.*

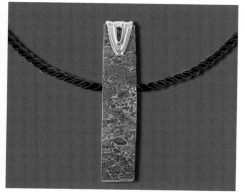

Fig. 5.13 Dinosaur gembone pendant design © Eve Alfillé. *Photo: Matthew Arden.*

Fig. 5.14 Dinobone double-sided pendant and photo by Tom DeGasperis of Dancing Designs.

Fig. 5.16 Rib bones probably from an allosaurus. *Photo by Barbara Eberle.*

Fig. 5.15 Mineralized legbone from some type of sauropod dinosaur embedded in conglomerate. *Photo by Barbara Eberle.*

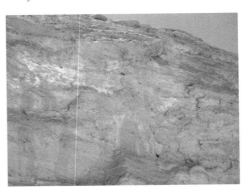

Fig. 5.18 The type of terrain in Utah where dino bones are found. *Photo by Barbara Eberle.*

Fig. 5.17 Dinosaur bone in conglomerate. *Photo by Barbara Eberle.*

Fig. 5.19 Diamond and gembone inlay ring by Mark Anderson. *Photo by Jessica Dow.*

Fig. 5.20 Dinosaur gembone carving by Martha Borzoni. *Photo by Jessica Dow.*

Most of the fossils occur in the green siltstone beds and lower sandstones, formed by the rivers and flood plains of the Jurassic period roughly 150–200 million years ago. Agatized dinosaur bone is also found in Southern Argentina and Chile. It is illegal to remove any fossil vertebrate bones from public land such as the Dinosaur National Monument in Utah and Colorado.

Agatized coprolite is found primarily in Utah, Colorado, Montana and Arizona. Non-gem material is found throughout the world. Some of the coprolite sold in the U.S. is from Madagascar. The largest coprolite is said to have been found in Saskatchewan, Canada. During the 19th century, coprolite was mined in England for industrial and military applications. Its high phosphate content made ground coprolite valuable for fertilizer, ammunition and explosives. Other countries have probably used coprolite in a similar manner. Since coprolite is a fossil, some countries have restrictions on exporting it in jewelry or rough form even when found on private land. Before you buy gembone or coprolite, verify first that it is legal. If you are a tourist, make sure you can export it.

Evaluation of Gembone & Pricing Ranges

The following factors affect the value of gembone:
- ◆ Color
- ◆ Intensity and brightness of the colors
- ◆ Number of colors
- ◆ Durability
- ◆ Cell size
- ◆ Cell pattern
- ◆ Type of bone (e.g., vertebras, hip, joint, etc.)
- ◆ Completeness of the bone
- ◆ Presence of agate fortifications
- ◆ Treatment quality

Color: According to gembone collector Mark Buford, bright canary yellow sells at a premium compared to other colors and it is usually the first to sell at rock shows. Green, red, orange and blue are also desirable colors. Red is the most common and stable of the bright gem grade colors. Gray, brown, beige and mustard colors are the lowest priced; nevertheless, they make attractive jewelry for people who like earth tones.

Black is the most sought-after color for the cell walls because it clearly defines the cells and provides high contrast. White is the second most desirable color for the webbing followed by dark brown, tan and other colors.

Intensity and brightness of the colors: Normally the brighter and more intense the color the more valuable the gembone. Some pastel colors such as pink or light blue may also be prized because of their rarity.

Number of colors: Single-colored gembone usually costs less than that which is multicolored. Nine colors is the magical maximum and most prized combination according to Mark Anderson, a jeweler who specializes in fine rare gems and gembone and who provided many photos and much of the information for this chapter.

Durability: The fewer the fractures and the less fragile the bone, the better its quality. The best gembone is chalcedony (cryptocrystalline quartz) because of its hardness (6.5–7 on the Mohs scale). Calcite gembone is much softer (Mohs 3), and consequently lower in price and durability. However, the presence of a little calcite helps create neon-like colors and a silver-sheen effect, which add beauty to the gembone.

Dinosaur Gembone from Different Seasons Jewelry
Photos by Mark Anderson

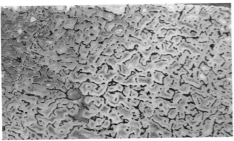

Fig. 5.21 Canary yellow and orange with black webbing (top color gembone and webbing)

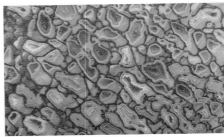

Fig. 5.22 Macro view of top-grade gembone with several colors including bright yellow

Fig. 5.23 Blue and red cab

Fig. 5.24 Red cab, black webbing

Fig. 5.25 Rare blue and green cab

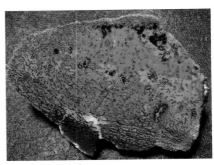

Fig. 5.26 Bright orange

Fig. 5.27 Bright pink rough

Fig. 5.28 Gemmy lavender and green

Dinosaur Gembone & Jewelry from Different Seasons Jewelry
Photos by Mark Anderson

Fig. 5.29 Top grade, nine colors

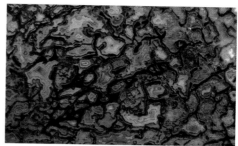

Fig. 5.30 Close-up of top grade nine colors

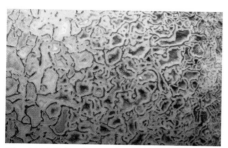

Fig. 5.31 Prized yellow gembone

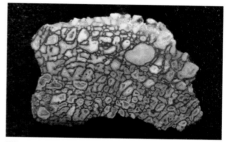

Fig. 5.32 Large-celled pink gembone

Fig. 5.33 Fanned cell pattern, large cells

Fig. 5.34 Vertebra with peacock pattern

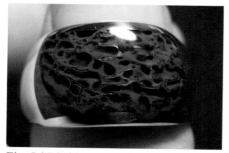

Fig. 5.35 Spiderweb pattern

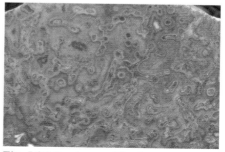

Fig. 5.36 Gembone with tube pattern

Mark Anderson advises, "If you have a very colorful gembone slab or jewelry piece, tilt it from side to side, front to back under a strong light, and look for a silver 'chatoyancy effect' to run across the stone. If you see a small or large white opaque pocket or area in bone or coprolite, check that area first under the light. In jewelry-grade bone, calcite lowers the price when it's set in a ring or bracelet due to durability issues."

Cell size: The larger the cells the higher the price, provided they are bright.

Cell pattern: Fanned cell patterns are desirable. According to jeweler Mark Anderson, the peacock vertebra pattern is the most valued. In fact it is so prized that collectors typically don't want to sell gembone with the pattern. Few dinosaurs had the peacock pattern in their vertebrae, and of those that had it, not all of their vertebrae displayed the rare and sought-after pattern. Some collectors consider it sacrilegious to cut such specimens up for jewelry.

Fig. 5.37 Bright contrasting colors, large cells, & fortifications add value to the gembone in these double-sided earrings by Mark Anderson of Different Seasons Jewelry. *Photo by Jessica Dow.*

A spiderweb pattern (fig. 5.35) is a good sign that the bone is durable. This can be a very high value pattern in bone but usually it lacks the color to make it jewelry-worthy. Because of its rarity, a tube pattern (fig. 5.36) almost always adds to the price of the gembone, all other factors being equal.

Type of bone (e.g., vertebra, hip, joint, etc.): Vertebrae are the highest priced and most collectable, particularly when they are matched pairs. The ends of large bones are also in demand because they tend to have large cells and are a good place to seek attractive patterns.

Completeness of bone: A complete vertebra or joint is more valuable than a partial one (fig. 5.39).

Presence of agate fortifications: Fortifications are areas in fractures and openings that are filled with banded agate. Amethyst, citrine or calcite crystals are sometimes at the center of the fortifications, while others have agate patterns. The larger and more colorful the agate pockets, the more valuable the dino bone.

Treatment quality: Top grade jewelry bone will have no treatment whatsoever other than the usual cutting and polishing of the bone. However, sometimes Opticon or Super T Gap Filling Glue is used to fill a fracture or void. Any stabilization of the material must be disclosed. Given an otherwise comparable piece, untreated gembone will be more highly valued. Collector specimens of dinosaur bone are usually stabilized because they are larger than jewelry pieces and must be as complete as possible to get top dollar. It is normal for dinosaur bones to have some fractures after being crushed by the earth under which they are buried. In order to hold the specimen together when it is cut and polished, fractures are filled with epoxy or Super Glue. If the stabilization treatment is successful, the bone will be more attractive and stable than when it came out of the ground. The more natural-looking the treatment is, the more value it adds to the collector specimens.

Dinosaur Gembone & Jewelry from Different Seasons Jewelry
Photos by Mark Anderson

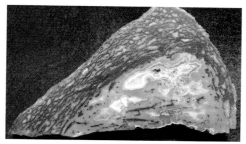

Fig. 5.38 Fortified blue gembone, tube pattern

Fig. 5.39 Complete vertebrae pair

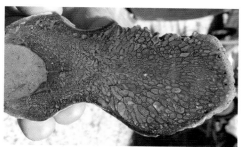

Fig. 5.40 Valuable nearly complete vertebra with peacock pattern. *Photo: Barbara Eberle.*

Fig. 5.41 Vertebra in fig. 5.40 close-up. *Photo by Barbara Eberle.*

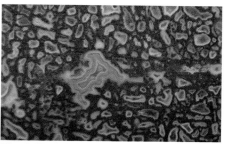

Fig. 5.42 Pink fortification in blue gembone

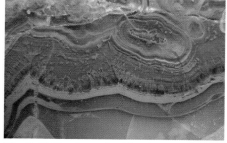

Fig. 5.43 Gembone fortification close-up

Fig. 5.44 Complete cell pattern

Fig. 5.45 Dino bone with pyrite

Dinosaur Gembone & Jewelry from Different Seasons Jewelry
Photos by Mark Anderson

Fig. 5.46 Medium grade dino bone

Fig. 5.47 Medium-high grade bone

Fig. 5.48 Low grade bone with drab color and voids in cells, which weaken the bone

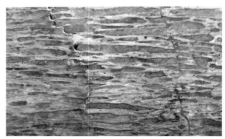

Fig. 5.49 Low grade bone with fractures and cell walls that won't take a high polish

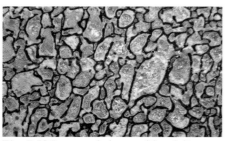

Fig. 5.50 Low grade bone with calcite

Fig. 5.51 Low grade bone with calcite

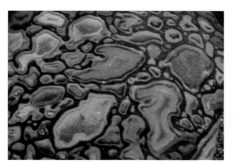

Fig. 5.52 Top grade gembone

Fig. 5.53 Dinobone chocolates

The most important value factors for gembone are color, brightness and the number of colors followed by hardness, cell size and pattern. Most gembone sold today is not investment quality, but much of it can be used to create distinctive jewelry.

As for the pricing of gembone, Mark Anderson says that a 20-mm round cab would cost about $5 if low grade, $15+ if medium grade and $100 and up for high grades. From his experience, canary yellow gembone has always received top dollar and is the most prized color among collectors. Even on eBay, slabs and cabs with this bright yellow color are the most popular. The mustard yellow bone, however, sells for very little; it has to be the neon yellow canary color to attract top dollar.

Evaluation of Coprolite & Pricing Ranges

The evaluation of coprolite is less complex than that of gembone. Color, brightness, pattern and durability are the key factors:

Color: Neon yellow, orange, or bright red are the most prized colors amongst collectors and jewelers. Brightness is also important. Brown and dull-looking colors are the lowest priced. However, some people like neutral beige or brown jewelry that can blend with much of their clothing.

Pattern: The presence of plant or animal tissue is desirable, and for some coprolite collectors, it is mandatory. Banded patterns are also prized. In general, multicolored patterned coprolite is more valuable than single color pieces.

Amount of agate; The larger the agate pockets, the prettier the coprolite, the greater the durability, and consequently the higher the price.

Fig. 5.54 Coprolite bolo tie and rough from Nevada Book & Mineral Company. *Photo © Renée Newman.*

Durability: The fewer and smaller the fractures, the better and more durable the coprolite. Perfect-fracture-free large and colorful agate pockets are extremely prized both in coprolite and dinosaur gembone.

Coprolite is low priced. The rough from Utah shown in figures 5.11 and 5.54 retail for about $20 per piece. Each rough specimen weighs roughly two pounds or one kilo. The belt buckle and bolo tie in those photos would cost about $75 each. If they were designer pieces, the price would be higher.

Dinosaur Gembone Imitations and Assembled Stones

Material sold as dinosaur gembone is not always accurately represented, particularly on the Internet. Be aware of the following potential impostors.

Quench-crackled and sugar- & acid-treated stones: These imitations consist of quench-crackled chalcedony that has been boiled in sugar and treated with acid to turn the sugar into carbon, making it black. The fractures are then treated to turn them white and give the appearance of black dinosaur bone with white webbing.

To finish the process, the stones are then tumbled, which breaks away some of the fracturing on the surface to give the undercut appearance that natural dinosaur bone displays. The "webbing" in this material looks nothing like the webbing in real dinosaur bone. It is broken up and jagged instead of smooth and circular. The undercutting on the imitation material is also very deep compared to its natural counterpart. Unfortunately, this treated chalcedony has been sold as authentic dinosaur bone.

Fig. 5.55 Imitation dino bone before and after treatment. *Photo © Mark Anderson.*

Fig. 5.56 Backside of imitation dino bone. *Photo © Mark Anderson.*

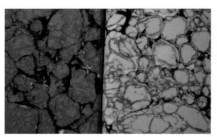 

Fig. 5.57 Composite dino bone. *Photo © Mark Anderson.*

Fig. 5.58 Doublet with petrified wood back. *Photo © Mark Anderson.*

Composite bone: Sometimes dinosaur bone that is too low in quality to be used in jewelry can be ground up, mixed with an epoxy resin, and colored. A cell pattern is then created to make it look like gembone (fig. 5.57). Since the material contains some bone matter, it can be called dinosaur bone composite. However, this product is commonly sold as dinosaur gembone and not as a composite. The material is often used in pens or knife handles, but is also found in jewelry, now that gembone is becoming more popular.

Doublets: Jewelry-grade dinosaur bone doublets come in two forms. The first type consists of extremely bright bone that is too fractured and soft to be used alone; it is topped with quartz or other type of clear cap. The second type of doublet is made by gluing very high quality gembone onto chalcedony or other material; the gembone is cut thin on top of the base so it can be domed, thereby maximizing the harvest of high quality bone.

A doublet can be hidden under a bezel so only the high quality dome top of the assembly is showing. Look underneath the setting to see if the bottom of the stone is the same as the top. An example of a doublet with a petrified wood base is shown in figure 5.58.

Dinosaur gembone allows designers to create unique jewelry that is attractive and an interesting conversation piece. It is an ideal gift for an orthopedist, osteoporosis specialist, paleontologist or anyone interested in prehistoric life. Deal with ethical sellers when purchasing dinosaur gembone. You can then be assured of selecting gembone that is both legal and genuine.

Caring for Dinosaur Gembone and Coprolite

Even though they are fossilized, dinosaur bone and coprolite are natural materials that may crack or warp when subjected to extreme temperatures or sudden changes from hot to cold. In addition, they may contain gem materials that require special care such as calcite and opal. Long exposure in direct sunlight and heat should be avoided. For example, do not place gembone in a sunny display case, leave it in a hot car, or wear it in a sauna. Even when swimming, it is best to take off your jewelry. Chlorine can gradually eat away at the metal alloy as well as bleach some of the gem materials found in dinosaur gembone or coprolite. Treated material is usually more susceptible to damage than that which is untreated. For example, quench-crackled chalcedony can chip more easily.

Clean your jewelry periodically with warm water and a mild liquid soap such as Ivory. Avoid ultrasonics, steam cleaners and chemicals such as acids, acetone or bleach. Proper care is essential for getting maximum enjoyment from your jewelry.

Metaphysical Properties of Dino Bone

Dino bone is a fossil—a preserved remnant of the past. Consequently it is used to help with past life regression and to provide a bridge to other worlds and other planes of existence. Shamans around the world still believe that fossils are valuable tools for amplifying magical energy.

In her book *Love is the Earth*, Melody says that dinosaur bone can open avenues of communication and insight, assisting one in understanding the changes in the earth, the role of evolution and issues of endurance. Dino bone also "facilitates mind travel, providing for a stabilizing force to ground the user while allowing the mind to wander toward a pre-set goal." In terms of health benefits, Melody says that dino bone can be used to help assimilate phosphorus within the body, to stimulate orderly growth of tissues, to control the temperature and release of fevers from the body, and to rebuild disarranged skeletal structures. Wearing dino bone can help prevent osteoporosis and slow the aging process, perhaps because it reminds the wearer of the need to develop good health habits.

Chalcedony, a common constituent of gembone, is a stone that enhances generosity, alleviates hostilities, dissipates negative thoughts, and balances the energy of the mind. Together, chalcedony and dino bone symbolize good will and promote benevolence and brotherhood among all.

6

Andalusite

Sometimes called the "poor man's alexandrite," andalusite often displays two distinct colors face up, which are usually yellowish green and orange. A third yellow color may also be visible. Unlike alexandrite, whose colors change when the lighting is switched from daylight to incandescent lighting, andalusite typically shows two colors simultaneously under the same light. This is because cutters generally orient andalusite to maximize its strong **pleochroism,** the property of certain minerals to exhibit different colors when viewed from different directions. The contrasting colors create a distinctive looking gemstone. Gem cuts with a long axis such as an oval or rectangle tend to show one color near the center and a second color near the ends; round cuts usually blend the colors into a mosaic, as shown in figures 6.1–6.3 below.

Figs. 6.1–6.3 Andalusites cut & photographed by Coast-to-Coast Rarestones International

Occasionally, andalusites are cut to emphasize just their orange or pink color (figs. 6.4–6.6). Flashes of olive green may also be visible.

Figs. 6.4–6.6 Andalusites cut & photographed by Coast-to-Coast Rarestones International

Andalusite is named after Andalusia, an autonomous community in Spain where it was first discovered. A bright green variety that is colored by manganese is called viridine or manganandalusite. A translucent variety that has graphite inclusions forming a cross shape is called chiastolite (fig. 6.7). The name is from the Greek *chiastos,* meaning "arranged diagonally" because the pattern of carbon inclusions resembles the Greek letter *chi,* which is written "χ." Chiastolite is sometimes cut and polished for amulets and charms in countries such as Spain, where the symbol of the cross has deep religious significance. Because of impurities, chiastolite may have a lower hardness and density than transparent stones.

g. 6.7 Andalusite crystals and faceted stones from Brazil; chiastolite from Australia. © *H. A. Hänni, EF Swiss Gemmological Institute.*

Geographic Sources of Andalusite

Most gem-grade andalusite is from Brazil in the States of Minas Gerais and Espirito Santo. Sri Lanka and Myanmar are minor sources. For detailed information on gem-quality andalusite from Brazil, consult the Summer 2009 issue of *Gems & Gemology* (pp 120–129).

Chiastolite is mined in South Australia, Spain, Siberia, Myanmar, Zimbabwe, and California, Pennsylvania and Maine in the U.S.. In recent years, large quantities of excellent chiastolite have been coming from Hunan Province, China.

South Africa, Kazakhstan, Korea and Mono County, California have been commercial sources of industrial grade andalusite. The material is used in the manufacture of spark plugs and other heat resistant porcelains.

Identifying Characteristics of Andalusite

Andalusite is an aluminum silicate with the chemical formula Al_2SiO_5, the same as that of kyanite and sillimanite. However, andalusite has a different crystal structure. Minerals that differ in crystal structure but have the same chemical composition are called **polymorphs**. Therefore, andalusite is a polymorph of kyanite and sillimanite, and all three are members of the sillimanite group.

Andalusite may be confused with chrysoberyl, topaz, tourmaline, sphene and vesuvianite. It can be separated from these minerals by its RI, birefringence, optic character and pleochroism, which is illustrated in figures 6.8–6.11. These and other properties are provided in Table 6.1.

Some inclusions found in andalusite are needles (typically rutile), apatite, hematite flakes, mica, fluid inclusions and sillimanite fibers (in stones from the Santa Teresa district, Espirito Santo, Brazil). Chiastolite has carbon inclusions.

Fig. 6.8 Pleochroism in andalusite, gamma and alpha rays shown. *Photo by Elise Skalwold.*

Figs. 6.9 & 6.10 Different views of the same andalusite looking through a London dichroscope. From one direction it is a brownish red, but when the Polaroid filter is moved, the gemstone turns colorless. *Photos by Robert James of the International School of Gemology.*

Table 6.1

Identifying Characteristics of Andalusite		
RI: 1.63–1.65	**SG:** 3.13–3.20 Lower for chiastolite	**Birefringence**: 0.007–0.013
Hardness: 6.5–7.5 Chiastolite: 5–5.5	**Dispersion**: 0.016	**Cleavage:** Distinct/good, good on {110}, poor on {100}.
Toughness: Fair–good	**Crystal System:** Orthorhombic	**Optic Char:** DR, biaxial -
Polish luster: Vitreous	**Fracture**: Uneven to subconchoidal with a vitreous luster	

Pleochroism: Strong with two or three pleochroic colors in green and orange stones. The three pleochroic colors are typically yellowish green, reddish brown, and yellow or green or colorless.

Spectrum: Not diagnostic, but may show clusters of fine lines around 485 nm to 518 nm, and around 550 nm.

Fluorescence: Inert to LW. Might fluoresce weak to moderate green to yellowish green under SW illumination.

Crystal habit (form): Occurs as slender prisms or as nearly square crystals capped with pyramids; most of the gem-grade material is found as waterworn pebbles.

Geological setting: Occurs in metamorphic rocks, usually slates and schists or gneiss.

Stability: Stable to heat unless liquid inclusions are present, stable to light, no reaction to chemicals.

Treatments: Normally none. It can be heat treated to improve its color, but this is seldom done

Most of the technical data in the above table was based on *Gems: Fourth Edition* by Robert Webster, *Color Encyclopedia of Gemstones (1987)* by Joel Arem, *GIA Gem Reference Guide,* the GIA *Gem Identification Lab Manual* (2005), www.mindat.org, the Gem A Diploma in Gemmology Course (2009), and *Dana's Manual of Mineralogy,* 18th Edition, Cornelius Hurlbut.

Fig. 6.11 Eye-visible pleochroism in a slice of chiastolite. *Photo by Elise Skalwold.*

Fig. 6.12 Chiastolite sphere from John White. *Photo © R. Newman.*

Fig. 6.13 Tanzanian andalusite rough and photo from New Era Gems.

Fig. 6.14 Scenic andalusite pendant from Devon Fine Jewelry. *Photo: Tony Seideman.*

Metaphysical Properties of Andalusite & Chiastolite

D. J. Conway, author of *Crystal Enchantments* suggests wrapping the stone in a small piece of dark green cloth and carrying it in your left-hand pocket, or pinning it inside your lingerie on the left side. "This helps bring in innovative ideas, strength and will power when working on a long-term. project that requires you to be on your toes at all times."

In *Love is in the Earth,* Melody says that andalusite helps you view the different facets of your emotional, physical, and intellectual character while allowing you to remain grounded and unbiased about the results. It can also encourage you to look at issues rationally and see the various sides to a problem or situation. In addition, andalusite stimulates the memory, promotes expertise in allegorical interpretation, and promotes the chivalrous aspects of ones character.

Chiastolite was used in ancient times to ward off curses. It is also said to lessen fevers, stimulate lactation, balance the immune system, and heal rheumatism and gout. In *The Crystal Bible,* Judy Hall states that psychologically, chiastolite dissolves illusions and calms fears; mentally it aids problem solving; and emotionally, it clears feelings of guilt and stabilizes the emotions.

Fig. 6.15 Andalusite. © *H. A. Hänni, SSEF Swiss Gemmological Institute.*

Fig. 6.16 Andalusite from Pala Gems International. *Photo by Mia Dixon.*

Evaluation of Andalusite & Pricing Ranges

It is difficult to find andalusite gems above three carats in weight and very difficult to find them above five carats. However, there are documented andalusites up to 40 carats in size. Despite its rarity and unique appearance, prices of andalusite are relatively low. Retail prices for extra fine andalusite above five carats seldom surpass $800 per carat. Low-quality material less than three carats may sell at prices below $20 per carat. The retail range of eye-clean andalusite about one carat in size is roughly $50 to $200 per carat.

In the opinion of dealer Simon Watt, the finest andalusite would be an "orange-brown and olive-green with flashes of pink, but preferences vary. The tone (lightness/darkness) and saturation (intensity) is more important than the actual hue (e.g., orange, yellow, green, pink, etc.). Very dark or very light stones generally cost less than more colorful ones in medium to medium-dark tones. Unlike stones such as sapphire, where pleochroism may be a negative factor, it is desirable for andalusite to display more than one color in the face-up position. In fact it is a feature that distinguishes andalusite from stones with similar colors.

Clarity and transparency are important factors that can determine whether a stone is industrial, commercial, or fine quality. Highly included material can sell for less than $5.00 per carat.

The quality of the cutting also affects price because good cutting requires more time and usually results in a greater loss of weight from the rough. But it is worth the additional cost because the end result of proper cutting is greater brilliance and a better display of color.

Caring for Andalusite

Andalusite is best cleaned with warm, soapy water and a soft cloth. The *GIA Gem Reference Guide* says that ultrasonics are usually safe, but the *Gem A Diploma in Gemmology Course* advises avoiding ultrasonics. A steamer is risky if liquid inclusions are present. With a hardness of 7–7.5, andalusite is relatively durable although it is slightly more brittle than other gems of similar hardness. In most cases, the cleavage does not present a problem. In other words, andalusite is a stone well suited for use in jewelry.

Kyanite

If you like sapphire and tanzanite, then you'll enjoy kyanite because it has similar colors. In fact, kyanite is occasionally found in parcels of sapphires. Its name is derived from the Greek *kyanos,* meaning "blue." Though kyanite is normally blue, it may also be green, yellow, orange, brown, gray, white or colorless. Blue varieties of kyanite are caused by the presence of iron combined with titanium, much like sapphire. That's why blue kyanite and sapphire are so similar in color. Green kyanite, by contrast, owes its color to vanadium.

Kyanite's original name was **cyanite**, which was given to it in 1789 by German geologist Abraham G. Werner. Much of the material actually has a blue-green color. **Disthene** is an alternate term for kyanite used by French writers.

A unique property of kyanite is its directional hardness. One direction along the crystal has a hardness of 4 to 5, but another direction at a right angle to that has a hardness of 6 to 7.5. The hardness variation is much like in wood—with the harder direction across the grain and the softer direction along with the grain. In kyanite crystals, a splintery grain direction is often visible that corresponds to the crystal axis. Diamond also has a marked directional hardness. It is this property of directional hardness that allows cutters to saw and facet diamonds. However, in the case of kyanite, the variability in hardness and its perfect cleavage make it challenging to cut and set.

Most kyanite in jewelry is fashioned as cabochons or beads, but transparent material is often faceted. Occasionally kyanite is cut as a cat's-eye cabochon.

Fig. 7.1 Kyanite crystals and faceted stones. © *H. A. Hänni, SSEF Swiss Gemmological Institute.*

Fig. 7.2 Kyanite necklace from Elaine Ferrari. *Photo © Renée Newman.*

Fig. 7.3 Kyanite and moonstone bracelet from Lang Antique & Estate Jewelry. *Photo by Thomas Picarella.*

Fig. 7.4 Green kyanite and Andean pink opal necklace. *Design copyright by Eve J. Alfillé; photo by Matthew Arden.*

Fig. 7.5 Blue and green kyanite earrings from Ear Charms Inc. *Photo © Renée Newman.*

Fig. 7.6 Kyanite specimen from Nevada Mineral and Book company. *Photo © Renée Newman.*

Fig. 7.8 Kyanite from Minas Gerais, Brazil. *Specimen and photo from Wright's Rock Shop.*

Fig. 7.7 Orange kyanite specimen and photo from New Era Gems.

Fig. 7.9 Kyanite (3.52 cts) from Nepal. *Pala Gems International; photo by Mia Dixon.*

Fig. 7.10 Kyanite (2.65 ct) cut & photographed by Robert Drummond of Mountain Lily Gems.

Fig. 7.11 Brazilian kyanite (3.75 ct) cut and photographed by Robert Drummond of Mountain Lily Gems.

Fig. 7.12 Brazilian Kyanite cut & photographed by Robert Drummond of Mountain Lily Gems.

Fig. 7.13 Brazilian kyanite (4.12 cts) cut and photographed by Coast-to-Coast Rarestones International.

Fig. 7.14 Brazilian green kyanite (2.29 cts) cut and photographed by Coast-to-Coast Rarestones International.

Geographic Sources of Kyanite

Transparent kyanite with a good blue color is found in several places—Brazil, Kenya, India, China, Tanzania, Mozambique, Myanmar, Nepal and USA (North Carolina). However, since about 2001, Nepal has been the most important source of top-grade blue kyanite, followed by Brazil. It is Nepali kyanite, that comes closest to imitating fine sapphire.

Industrial grade material occurs more widely in the above-mentioned countries and is also found in Switzerland, Italy, Russia, Australia and various states in the U.S., including Massachusetts, Connecticut, Georgia, Virginia, and Vermont. Industrial kyanite is used to produce spark-plugs, electrical insulators, abrasives, porcelain dishware and plumbing fixtures. India is the largest producer of industrial-use kyanite.

Metaphysical Properties of Kyanite

Kyanite is a stone of tranquility, which stimulates psychic awareness on all levels and never accumulates negative energy or vibrations. Blue kyanite is useful for performers and public speakers because it is said to strengthen the voice and heal the throat and larynx. If you sleep with kyanite, it is supposed to promote dream solving by helping you recall your dreams and by making them more lucid. Kyanite can assist in negotiations, diplomatic missions, arbitration and other forms of communication between disharmonious people by acting as an energetic bridge.

Crystal healers use kyanite to help:

♦ Relieve pain
♦ Lower blood pressure
♦ Heal infections
♦ Reduce excess weight
♦ Bridge the energy gaps caused by bone breakage or surgery
♦ Reestablish neural pathways after head trauma, seizures or strokes
♦ Calm the nerves

Identifying Characteristics of Kyanite

Kyanite is an aluminum silicate with the chemical formula Al_2SiO_5, the same as that of andalusite and sillimanite. However, kyanite has a different crystal structure. Minerals that differ in crystal structure but have the same chemical composition are called **polymorphs**. Therefore, kyanite is a polymorph of andalusite and sillimanite, and all three are members of the sillimanite group.

Often kyanite is easy to distinguish from other stones because of its fibrous appearance, color zoning and white streaks (figs. 7.15 and 7.16). However, transparent eye-clean material may be confused with sapphire, tanzanite, spinel, aquamarine benitoite, and iolite. Refractive index, pleochroism, spectrum and birefringence will separate kyanite from other gems. Mineralogists can use its directional hardness to confirm that the rough is kyanite—a knife can scratch it parallel to the crystal length but not across. In addition, the bladed tabular crystals are quite distinctive so its identification is typically easy. Details about the physical and optical properties of kyanite are provided in Table 7.1.

Fig. 7.15 Kyanite pendant. © Newman.

Fig. 7.16 Close-up view of the fibrous kyanite in fig. 7.15. *Photo © Renée Newman.*

Table 7.1

Identifying Characteristics of Kyanite		
RI: 1.710—1.734	**SG**: 3.53–3.70	**Birefringence**: 0.012–0.017 (Cr-kyanite up to 0.033)
Hardness: 4–5 in one direction, 6–7.5 at 90° to it.	**Dispersion**: 0.020	**Cleavage**: Perfect in one direction, distinct in one direction, parting.
Toughness: Fair–poor	**Crystal System**: Triclinic **Optic Char**: DR: the optic sign for kyanite is nearly neutral, some appears positive and others negative.	
Polish luster: Vitreous	**Fracture**: Uneven, splintery with a vitreous to pearly luster	
Pleochroism: Moderate pleochroism. Usually dark blue, colorless, and violet-blue.		
Spectrum: Often shows iron bands at 435 nm and 445 nm in the violet. Stones that contain chromium might show faint, fine lines at 652 nm, 671 nm, and 689 nm in the red.		
Fluorescence: Some kyanite shows weak red fluorescence under LW.		
Crystal habit (form): Columnar, bladed, tabular, flattened, elongated.		
Geological setting: Occurs in schists, gneiss, and granite pegmatites.		
Stability: Very sensitive to heat; stable to light; not attacked by acids.		
Treatments: Normally none, but some material is heated and fracture filling is possible.		

Most of the technical data in the above table was based on *Gems: Fourth Edition* by Robert Webster, *Color Encyclopedia of Gemstones (1987)* by Joel Arem, *GIA Gem Reference Guide,* www.mindat.org, the GIA *Gem Identification Lab Manual* (2005), the Gem A Diploma in Gemmology Course (2009) of the British Gemmological Association, *Dana's Manual of Mineralogy,* 18th Edition, Cornelius Hurlbut, and *Gems & Gemology,* Spring 2002, pp 96 & 97.

Fig. 7.17 Kyanite bracelet. *Jewelry and photo from Charles Albert, Inc.*

Fig. 7.18 Kyanite earrings. *Jewelry and photo from Charles Albert, Inc.*

Fig. 7.19 Kyanite earrings. *Design copyright by Eve J. Alfillé; photo by Matthew Arden.*

Fig. 7.20 Strands of kyanite beads from Bear Essentials. *Photo by Bear Williams.*

Evaluation of Kyanite & Pricing Ranges

One of the biggest advantages of kyanite is its affordable price. Gem quality kyanite is far more rare than tanzanite or sapphire and it can have similar beauty, yet it costs significantly less. For example, the 5.38-carat blue kyanite in figure 7.21 would retail for between $200–$300 per carat as of the publication date of this book. That is despite the fact that it is extremely difficult to find evenly colored kyanites with such a high clarity in sizes above five carats.

With the exception of material from Nepal, most transparent kyanite is heavily included. The lower the clarity, the lower the price. You can find commercial quality kyanite for less than $50 per carat.

Fig. 7.21 Kyanite from Nepal (5.38 cts). *Photo by Bear Williams of Stone Group Laboratories.*

Translucent and fibrous kyanite sells for less than $15 per carat and is used to create distinctive jewelry pieces. Semi-opaque material that is like rock may cost a few dollars or less per stone or it may be sold by the strand as a necklace. Strands of commercial quality kyanite beads are available for less than $100, but expect to pay more if the strands are transparent. For example, the strands in figure 7.20 retail for around $300 per strand.

An intense sapphire blue color is generally the most in demand, but other kyanite colors can also be attractive. Very dark or very light stones generally cost less than more colorful ones in medium to medium-dark tones. Vibrant colors with as little gray as possible fetch the highest prices.

Try to select a stone that displays color all across the stone instead of one showing a washed out window area in the center. In so doing, you will be visually judging cut. Expect to pay more for well-cut stones that maximize brilliance over weight. The majority of stones in fine color will be cut shallow to maximize yield from the blade-like crystals.

Caring for Kyanite

Clean kyanite with warm soapy water and a soft cloth. Avoid ultrasonics and steam cleaners. Kyanite is not a good ring stone for everyday wear because of its directional hardness and perfect cleavage. Nevertheless, it can be worn in rings if it is set low and has a protective setting such as a bezel. Do not use metal tweezers on kyanite because they may scratch the stone. Instead use your fingers to hold loose stones. Kyanite is best worn in necklaces, earrings and brooches, where it is not subjected to hard knocks and where its beauty is easily visible.

8

Sillimanite

S illimanite was first described in 1824 for an occurrence in Chester, Connecticut. It was named after Benjamin Silliman, founder of the American Journal of Science and Professor of Chemistry and Geology at Yale University in New Haven, Connecticut. A common variety of sillimanite is known as **fibrolite**, because of its fibrous nature. If the fibers are straight and parallel, a cat's-eye effect may result when cut as a cabochon; radiating fibers can create a star. Fibrous material may be white, gray, black, brown, yellow or grayish, green.

Sillimanite may also be clear and free of eye-visible inclusions, and then it is usually faceted. The colors are typically blue, green, yellow, gray or colorless. Frequently, the tones are light to very light. In fact, the stones are often so light, that sillimanite has occasionally been used as a diamond substitute. However, darker tones are also available.

Rarer than andalusite and kyanite, sillimanite is primarily a collector's stone, nevertheless, it is also mounted in jewelry. In 1977, sillimanite even managed to achieve status as the state mineral of Delaware, where it has been found.

Fig. 8.1 Sillimanite earrings. *Design © by Eve J. Alfillé; Photo by Matthew Arden.*

Fig. 8.2 Sillimanite. © *H. A. Hänni, SSEF Swiss Gemmological Institute.*

Fig. 8.3 Sillimanite (8.21 cts) from *Pala Gems International; photo by Mia Dixon.*

Fig. 8.4 Sri Lankan sillimanite (4.07 cts) & photo from Coast-to-Coast Rarestones International.

Fig. 8.5 Sillimanite cat's-eyes from Blue Moon Enterprise. *Photo © Renée Newman.*

Fig. 8.6 Sillimanites, yellow from India, blue from Sri Lanka. © *H. A. Hänni, SSEF Swiss Gemmological Institute.*

Geographic Sources of Sillimanite

Myanmar, particularly the Mogok area, is noted for its fine quality blue and violet sillimanite, as well as ruby, sapphire and jade. Sri Lanka and especially India produce much of the cat's-eye sillimanite that is on the market as well as other gem varieties. Other sources of sillimanite include Kenya, Tanzania, Brazil, South Africa, Australia, Madagascar, Korea, Canada, Germany, France, Czechoslovakia, Scotland and several states in the U.S. including Connecticut, Delaware, New Hampshire, New Jersey, Pennsylvania, North Carolina, South Carolina, Idaho, South Dakota, and Oklahoma. Most of the sillimanite found is industrial grade and used in the manufacture of heat resistant ceramics and spark plugs. Sillimanite is also used as an index mineral indicating high temperature metamorphism.

Identifying Characteristics of Sillimanite

Sillimanite is an aluminum silicate with the chemical formula Al_2SiO_5, the same as that of andalusite and kyanite. However, sillimanite has a different crystal structure. Minerals that differ in crystal structure but have the same chemical composition are called **polymorphs**. Therefore, sillimanite is a polymorph of andalusite and kyanite, and all three are members of the sillimanite group.

Transparent sillimanite may be confused with spodumene, chrysoberyl, euclase, beryl and near colorless varieties of other minerals. Refractive index (RI), specific gravity (SG), spectrum, fluorescence, and magnification are used to help identify sillimanite. Under magnification, there may be very fine needles parallel to the cleavage direction, three directional needles, crystals and/or "fingerprints."

Green aggregate sillimanite may resemble jadeite or nephrite jade. Refractive index and specific gravity will separate sillimanite from nephrite; the spectrum and specific gravity can separate it from jadeite.

Cat's-eye sillimanite may be mistaken for other chatoyant varieties such as those of quartz, tourmanline, apatite, diopside, kornerupine, enstatite, and actinolite. RI, SG, spectrum, polariscope reaction, birifringence blink, and magnification help distinguish these gemstones from cat's-eye sillimanite. Most sillimanites do not fluoresce and if they do, it is usually a weaker fluorescence.

Details about the physical and optical properties of sillamanite are provided in Table 8.1 below:

Table 8.1

Identifying Characteristics of Sillimanite		
RI: 1.657—1.680	**SG**: 3.14–3.25	**Birefringence**: 0.015–0.021
Hardness: 7.5, but 6–7 for fibrous material	**Dispersion**: 0.015	**Cleavage**: Perfect in one direction
Toughness: Fair–poor	**Crystal System**: Orthorhombic	**Optic Char**: DR, biaxial +; AGG
Fracture: Splintery, uneven	**Polish luster**: Silky when fibrous, vitreous otherwise	
Pleochroism: Strong; in blue stones, colorless, light yellow, and blue; otherwise may be pale green, light green and blue or colorless, pale brown and yellow.		
Spectrum: Weak bands at 410 NM, 441 NM, and 462 NM.		
Fluorescence: Blue sillimanite shows weak red fluorescence under LW and SW.		
Crystal habit (form): Long slender crystals without distinct terminations, fine needles arranged in compact parallel groups, waterworn clear gemmy pebbles, or more frequently as fibrous masses.		
Geological setting: Occurs in schist, gneiss, and contact metamorphic rock.		
Stability: Sensitive to heat; stable to light; not attacked by acids.		
Treatments: Normally none, but fracture filling is possible. Fibrous sillimanite may be dyed to imitate more expensive stones such as ruby and emerald.		

Most of the technical data in the above table was based on *Gems: Fourth Edition* by Robert Webster, *Color Encyclopedia of Gemstones (1987)* by Joel Arem, *GIA Gem Reference Guide,* www.mindat.org, the GIA *Gem Identification Lab Manual* (2005), the Gem A Diploma in Gemmology Course (2009), *Handbook of Gem Identification* by Richard T. Liddicoat, and *Dana's Manual of Mineralogy,* 18th Edition, Cornelius Hurlbut.

Fig. 8.7 Sillimanite earrings. *Design copyright by Eve J. Alfillé; photo by Matthew Arden.*

Fig. 8.8 Sillimanite cat's-eye cross pendant from Lang Antique & Estate Jewelry. *Photo by Thoma Picarella.*

Evaluation of Sillimanite & Pricing Ranges

The best quality sillimanite can retail for up to $400 per carat. Sizes Low-grade stones are available for less than $10 per carat. Cat's-eye sillimanites generally retail for less than $100 per carat and are often available for less than $30 per carat. Information on assessing the quality of cat's-eye stones is provided in Chapter 3, "Cat's-eye Chrysoberyl."

Most sillimanite gems are below five carats, but they are also available in sizes between five and ten carats. Occasionally, sillimanites up to 20 carats are cut.

In general, blue sillimanite fetches the highest prices, The more intense the color, the higher the price. Yellow and colorless stones are also in demand. Clarity, transparency and cut quality can have a significant impact on their price.

Caring for Sillimanite

Clean sillamanite with warm soapy water and a soft cloth. Avoid ultrasonics and steam cleaners. Sillimanite is not a good ring stone for everyday wear because of its perfect cleavage. Nevertheless, it can be worn in rings if it is set low and has a protective setting such as a bezel. Sillimanite is best worn in necklaces, earrings and brooches.

Common Opal

Opals are the tears shed by Tonatiuh, the Sun God, many ages ago, and which fell upon the earth and have lodged in its bosom, turning into jewels. It was prophesied by our forefathers that men would labor wearily for them and kings would pay great price of gold therefor. Hence it is well to know the virtues and portents of these stones, and may wise men ponder deeply upon what I, Chimapopotl, a descendant of the high priest, will say. Now, some [of these stones] are white, though veined with red when held to the light, and these portend love and death . . . and there are some that shimmer with the blue of Heaven, and these speak of love . . . passion rings loud in those that are of the hue of gold.

Extract from an ancient Nahuatl manuscript in Querétaro, Mexico

The Mayas and Aztecs called opal the *Quetzal-itzlipyollitli* (bird of paradise stone) or *Vitzitziltecpatl* (hummingbird stone) in reference to the multicolored glistening plumage of these tropical birds. The Romans called opal *cupid paederos* (child beautiful as love) and revered it as the symbol of hope and purity. According to an Australian legend, the creator descended to Earth on a rainbow to bring the message of peace, and at the spot, where his foot touched the ground, the stones became alive and started sparkling in all the colors of the rainbow.

Historically, opal was considered a stone of good fortune that brought success, happiness and good health to its wearer. Therefore, it is surprising that a superstition emerged that opals brought bad luck. George Frederick Kunz, a famous American mineralogist and vice-president of Tiffany's, attributes this belief to a misunderstanding of a novel in which an enchanted opal was worn by one of the characters:

"There can be little doubt that much of the modern superstition regarding the supposed unlucky quality of the opal owes its origin to a careless reading of Sir Walter Scott's novel, *Anne of Geierstein*. The wonderful tale therein . . . contains nothing to indicate that Scott meant to represent the opal as unlucky."

The Curious Lore of Precious Stones (p 143) by George F. Kunz

The ancient Latin name for opal was *opalus*, which was probably derived from the Sanskrit *upala* meaning "precious stone." The Greek word for opal, *opállios*, means "to see a change (of color)." It has also been suggested that *opalus* could have come from the name of the Roman goddess of abundance and fertility, Opis, the wife of Saturn whose festival was called Opalia.

White opal was probably first mined at Czerwenitza, near Dubnik, Slovakia (formerly Hungary). Archival evidence shows that this mine was in operation in the 14th century, but it most likely was worked much earlier. In Mexico, fire opal was probably known to the Aztecs as early as the 13th century. The first unrecorded discovery of opal in Australia is said to be in 1849; the first recorded find was in 1872 at Listowel Downs in central Queensland (Gem A Diploma Course). Today the greatest proportion of the world's precious opal comes from Australia. Opal is the alternate birthstone for October and the 14th wedding anniversary stone.

Classification of Opal

Opal can be classified into three basic categories. In their 2009 *Diploma in Gemmology Course*, Gem A (the British Gemmological Association) divides opals into three basic categories:

◆ **Precious opal** — Opal with play-of-colour on a pale or dark background. This category includes black opal, boulder opal, white opal with play-of-color, water opal (crystal opal) and matrix opal (opal embedded in its host rock or displaying patches or veins of the rock in which it was found). /

◆ **Fire opal** — Transparent to translucent brownish-yellow, to orange, to reddish orange; may show a play-of-colour and be called precious fire opal

◆ **Common opal** — Translucent to opaque material with a range of body colors but no play-of-colour.

Some trade members avoid the use of the term "precious" as a category name because it suggests that stones outside of the category are not valuable, which is false. The term "common opal" is also disputed. Translucent blue opals and green opals with an even color are not easy to find, and they can make beautiful jewelry. Nevertheless, "common opal" is a convenient category name that encompasses all opals without a play-of-color that do not have a red to orange body color. Yellow stones have a transitional color, which leads them to be considered as common opal or fire opal depending on the situation.

This book focuses on common opal and fire opal because there is a need for more information about them. Several excellent books have been written on Australian opal and I featured it in my *Gemstone Buying Guide*. Rather than repeating what has already been written, I would rather add new material to the existing literature.

This chapter will discuss the various types of common opal, their geographic sources, qualities, metaphysical lore and prices. You'll learn about fire opals in Chapter 10. In addition, that chapter will outline the identifying properties of all opals and methods used to treat them or assemble them into triplets.

Types of Common Opal

Common opal is sometimes described as worthless opal because it has no play-of-color. But don't let that deceive you into thinking it has no value. Even the white or gray variety, the most widespread common opal, may be used for beads and other forms of jewelry or decorative items. It is found in Australia, North America, Central America, South America, Africa, Europe, and some parts of Asia. Common opal is often fluorescent and collected by mineral enthusiasts for that reason. Compared to chalcedony and quartz, which are also composed of silica, opal of like quality generally costs more per carat, particularly in the colored varieties.

Fig. 9.1 Opals without play-of-color. *Opals from Gerald Stockton; photo © Renée Newman.*

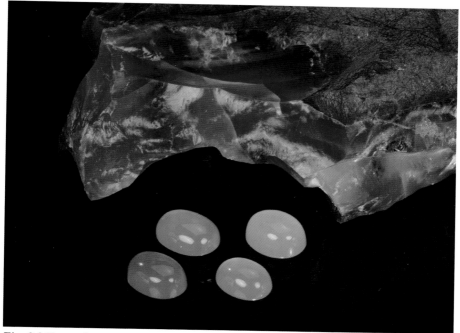

Fig. 9.2 Tanzanian prase opal from Pala Gems International. *Photo: Jason Stephenson.*

Fig. 9.3 Common opal (potch) beads. *Photo ©
Renée Newman.*

Fig. 9.4 Botryoidal opal from Mil-
ford, Utah. *Photo by Shoulin Lee.*

Fig. 9.5 Kosevo, Serbian green opal rough
from Emil Weis Opals. *Photo Tanja Schütz.*

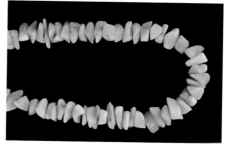

Fig. 9.6 Green Serbian opal beads from
Emil Weis Opals. *Photo by Tanja Schütz.*

When opal is carved or mounted in jewelry, it takes on another dimension that goes beyond per carat value. Designers may spend months looking for the right color and quality of opal and creating a design that will bring out its beauty. Some of the jewelry they create with "common opal" becomes museum pieces. Hopefully, the photos in this book will increase your appreciation of opal that does not feature a play-of-color.

Potch is another term used to refer to common opal, but normally it is reserved for opaque and milky white, grey, or black opal, which was found in the precious opal fields of Australia. "Magpie" potch is made up of black and white patches. The rest of this section will discuss other varieties of opal, which include pink, green, blue, yellow, colorless, cat's eye, dendritic, landscape, wood opal and banded opal.

The surface of some common opal is occasionally shaped like a bunch of grapes with rounded spheres. This material is called **botryoidal opal** and can be cut into interesting cabochons with one side resembling bubbles in a pot of boiling water (fig. 9.3). "Potch" and "botryoidal" are terms that can be applied to various colors of common opal. Varietal classifications of specific common opals are listed below:

Green opal: This nickle-bearing variety is a green translucent to semi-opaque opal that resembles chrysoprase or jade. It is commonly called **prase opal** or **prasopal**, perhaps because of its resemblance to chrysoprase, whose name is derived from Greek for "golden + leek." The refractive index and specific gravity of opal are significantly lower than that of chrysoprase so the two stones can easily be separated.

The two most important sources of green opal have been Tanzania and Serbia (a republic comprising most of the former Yugoslavia) but Tanzania is currently the most productive area. Green opal is also found in Peru, Poland, Oregon and California. Brazil is a source of a green cat's-eye variety. Figures 9.7 and 9.8 show the bottom and top range of quality and retail price of green opal—$1 per carat to about $150 per carat for a beautiful emerald green opal.

Fig. 9.7 Poor quality green opal. *Photo © Renée Newman.*

Fig. 9.8 High quality green opal from Pala Gems. *Photo by Jason Stephenson.*

Pink opal: Most pink opal is from Peru high up in the Andes Mountains. One locality is the Acari copper mining area near Arequipa, Peru. It has never been produced in great quantities, and since around 2008, the amount of pink opal available has been decreasing.

Fig. 9.9 Serbian opal earrings by Paula Crevoshay. *Photo by Chris Chavez.*

Fig. 9.10 Serbian opal ring by Paula Crevoshay. *Photo by Chris Chavez.*

Fig. 9.11 Prasopal rough from Hanety Hills, Dodoma, Tanzania. *Opal rough courtesy Emil Weis Opals; photo by Tanja Schütz.*

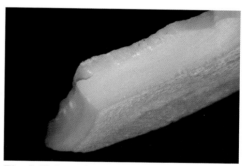

Fig. 9.12 Peruvian pink opal rough. *Photo by Wolf Kuehn/ Canadian Institute of Gemmology.*

Fig. 9.13 Peruvian opal pendant carved by Sherris Cottier Shank. *Photo: Amy Balthrop.*

Fig. 9.14 Peruvian pink opal earrings by Paula Crevoshay. *Photo: Chris Chavez.*

The Spencer mine in Idaho has also produced pink opal. Nevertheless, pink opal is so closely associated with Peru that some people simply call it Peruvian opal or Andean opal. However, blue and green opal are also found in Peru. Finding evenly colored translucent pink opal without dark inclusions is a challenge; therefore, expect to pay considerably more for pink opal such as that in figures 9.12–9.15 than for low quality pink opal. The rarity of pink opal also makes it more expensive than stones such as chalcedony, rose quartz and pink aventurine (a quartz rock). For example, the bracelet-length strand of poor quality opal beads in figure 9.16 cost $22, whereas the necklace-length strand of rose quartz and pink aventurine beads cost about $12. The faceting of the opal beads adds somewhat to the cost, but in general you should expect to pay at least double for pink opal beads and several times more for fine quality pink opal beads than for quartz or aventurine beads. Chapter 10 provides information on how to distinguish opal from stones that resemble it.

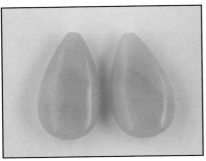

Fig. 9.15 Fine, well-matched pink opal cabs from Nazca, Peru. *Opals from Emil Weis Opals; photo by Tanja Schütz.*

Fig. 9.16 Top: pink aventurine, middle: rose quartz, poorly matched low-quality pink opal beads. *Photo © Renée Newman.*

Blue opal: Like green and pink opal, blue opal is relatively rare. Most of it is mined at high altitudes along with copper in the Andes Mountains near San Patricio, Peru. The green-blue color of Peruvian opal is frequently compared to that of the Caribbean Sea (figs. 9.17– 9.18). Depending on how the rough is cut, it can have a single translucent color, a multicolored scenic design or a dendritic fern-like pattern. Translucent even-colored green-blue qualities fetch the highest prices of all common opals. Dealers compare the top color to that of a high-quality paraiba tourmaline.

Fig. 9.17 Andean blue opals courtesy Emil Weis Opals. *Photo by Tanja Schütz.*

Fig. 9.18 Andean blue opal rough from Nazca Peru courtesy Emil Weis Opals. *Photo by Tanja Schütz.*

Fig. 9.19 Andean pink opal (10 mm) necklace design © Eve Alfillé. *Photo: Matthew Arden.*

Fig. 9.20 Andean blue opal necklace design © Eve J. Alfillé. *Photo: Matthew Arden.*

Oregon has also produced blue opal primarily at Opal Butte in Morrow County, but the color is more blue and less green and the material is semi-opaque (fig. 9.23).

Blue opal from Salto do Jacuí in the state of Rio Grande do Sul, Brazil is shown in figure 9.21. The blue variety has also been found in Idaho and British Columbia.

Fig. 9.21 Brazilian blue opal and photo from Wolf Kuehn.

Yellow opal: Yellow opal ranges from a brownish to golden to lemon yellow color and may be transparent to translucent (figs. 9.27–9.29). The price of yellow opal is generally less than that of orange to red fire opals of similar size, clarity, transparency and cut quality. Yellow opal is rarer than white and colorless opal but more widely available than pink, blue and green opal. It is found in Mexico, Brazil, Mali, Tanzania and the U.S. in the states of Oregon, Idaho and California. Some greenish yellow material from Mali is called lime opal (fig. 9.30).

Hyalite: Hyalite is a water clear opal with no play-of-color and is completely transparent. The name comes from the Greek word *hyalos* meaning glass. The main source is in the Czech Republic near Valec. It normally fluoresces a brilliant yellow-green due to trace elements of uranium. Most of the time, the rough looks like glass bubbles.

Dendritic opal (moss opal): This is common opal that has black mossy or fernlike patterns (dendrites), which are formed from inclusions of manganese oxide or other impurities. It can have various body colors and is usually translucent to semiopaque. Moss opal occurs in various localities including Serbia, Peru, Oregon, California and Western Australia.

Wood opal (opalized wood): This is wood that has been replaced with opal, or essentially, petrified wood with the structure of opal. The vitreous fracture luster of wood opal helps differentiate it from ordinary petrified wood, whose fracture surface has a duller waxy luster. One of the most important sources of wood opal is Slovakia, where it is found in more than 50 localities. The Virgin Valley of Nevada is another well-known source of wood opal. This variety is also found in

Fig. 9.22 Moss opal from Devon Fine Jewelry. *Photo by Tony Seideman.*

Bulgaria, British Columbia, Burundi, France, and the states of California, Colorado and Georgia. An example of wood opal with play-of-color is shown in figure 9.32.

Cat's-eye opal. Some opal cabochons reflect a band of light as the stone is moved. These are called cat's-eyes and may have various body colors (figs. 9.33–9.35).

Banded opal (includes onyx opal and agate opal): This is common opal that consists of layers of different colors of opal, or it may be layered with minerals such as chalcedony and quartz. The layers display a banded effect similar to onyx and agate (figs. 9.36–9.38). The Spencer mine in Idaho is particularly noted for its banded opal, but this distinctive variety is found in other localities as well.

Fig. 9.23 Oregon opal carved by Sherris Cottier Shank. *Photo; Amy Balthrop.*

Fig. 9.24 Peruvian blue opal pendant by Zaffiro. *Photo by Daniel Van Rossen.*

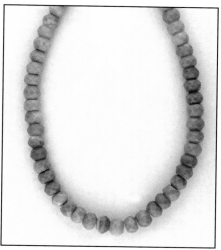

Fig. 9.25 Blue opal beads from Oregon. *Emil Weis Opals; photo by Tanja Schütz.*

Fig. 9.26 Opal beads from Nazca Peru. *Emil Weis Opals; photo by Tanja Schütz.*

Fig. 9.27 Yellow opal from Kayes, Mali. *Emil Weis Opals; photo by Tanja Schütz.*

Fig. 9.28 Yellow opal from Paula Crevoshay. *Photo: Chris Chavez.*

Fig. 9.29 Brazilian opal carved by Sherris Cottier Shank. *Photo by Amy Balthrop.*

Fig. 9.30 Lime opal from Kayes, Mali. *Emil Weis Opals; photo by Tanja Schütz.*

Fig. 9.31 Tanzanian golden opal beads. *Emil Weis Opals; photo by Tanja Schütz.*

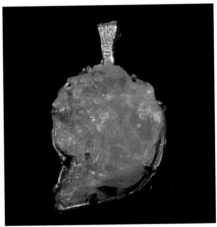

Fig. 9.32 Wood opal pendant from Idaho Opal & Gem Corp. *Photo: Tony Seideman.*

Fig. 9.33 Cat's-eye opal from Senhor de Pamfir, Bahia, Brazil. *Emil Weis Opals; photo by Tanja Schütz.*

Fig. 9.34 Cat's-eye opal rough from Senhor de Pamfir, Bahia, Brazil. *Emil Weis Opals; photo by Tanja Schütz.*

Fig. 9.35 Cat's-eye opal beads. *Emil Weis Opals; photo by Tanja Schütz.*

Fig. 9.36 Agate opal cabochons courtesy Paula Crevoshay. *Photo by Chris Chavez.*

Fig. 9.37 *Banded opal rough from Cedar City, Utah. Emil Weis Opals; photo by Tanja Schütz.*

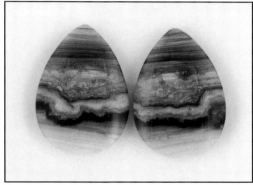

Fig. 9.38 *Banded opal cabochons from Cedar City, Utah. Emil Weis Opals; photo: Tanja Schütz.*

Fig. 9.39 Landscape opal from Acari, Peru. *Emil Weis Opals; photo by Tanja Schütz.*

Fig. 9.40 Landscape opal rough from Acari, Peru. *Emil Weis Opals; photo by Tanja Schütz.*

Fig. 9.41 An array of opal beads from Emil Weis Opals. Left to right: light opal from Australia, pink opal from Peru, boulder opal from Australia, blue opal from Peru, yellow opal from Tanzania, green opal from Serbia, boulder opal from Australia, fire opal from Mexico, fluorite opal from Utah, blue opal from Peru, picture opal from Peru, and blue opal from Oregon. *Photo by Tanja Schütz.*

Landscape opal, picture opal: Common opal with inclusions and varying color of opal can form images that look like landscapes, and when cut as beads, may look like miniature globes (9.39 and 9.42). These opals are appropriately called landscape opals. Much of the material comes from Peru, but Oregon is another source.

Fig. 9.42 Landscape opal (Acari, Peru) necklace from Emil Weis Opals. *Photo by Tanja Schütz.*

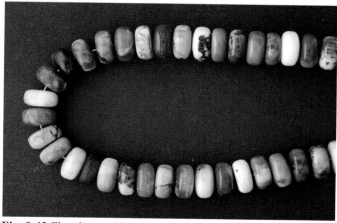

Fig. 9.43 Fluorite opal beads from Utah. *Emil Weis Opals; photo by Tanja Schütz.*

Fluorite opal, opalized fluorite, Tiffany stone, bertrandite: This unusual stone is composed mostly of opalized fluorite with other minerals such as quartz, chalcedony, manganese, and beryl (figs. 9.44 & 9.45). Though it is sometimes called bertrandite, that mineral is not the major constituent of the stone. Found in the west desert of Utah where beryllium is mined, fluorite opal most often has purple, blue black, and white patterns, some of which resemble Tiffany glass, hence the name Tiffany stone. Technically, fluorite opal is not common opal. Nevertheless it is a popular stone at gem and mineral shows and is typically found at the booths of opal dealers. Even though it has no play-of-color, fluorite opal is a colorful stone that is ideal for one-of-a-kind pieces.

Fig. 9.45 Fluorite opal rough from Delta, Utah. *Emil Weis Opals. Photo: Tanja Schütz.*

Fig. 9.44 Fluorite opal jewelry from Dreaming Down Under. *Photo © Renée Newman.*

Metaphysical Properties of Opal

In ancient Greece, the opal was said to induce mystical visions and help people foretell the future. In India, they would pass an opal across the brow to clear the brain and strengthen the memory. Opal has always been associated with love and passion; it is a seductive stone that intensifies emotional states and releases inhibitions. Wearing opal is said to bring loyalty, faithfulness and spontaneity.

White common opal is well suited for sensitive people who are easily overwhelmed by more powerful stones or for those who are overburdened with stress and need stones that will help them relax. White opal can attract angels and is an ideal gift to leave for them in an inconspicuous spot.

Pink opal is supposed to be a good stone for meditating, healing the emotions, and renewing spiritual relationships. Sleeping with pink opal helps one resolve painful remembrances and release old negative patterns.

Green opal is used to promote a relaxed state similar to meditation that can aid one in solving problems. It assists in rational fasting and in cleansing of the body internally to promote rejuvenation. It is said to strengthen the immune system and alleviate colds and flu.

Blue opal is an emotional soother and confidence builder. It is used to stimulate communications skills and to help people voice thoughts they have not been courageous enough to voice in the past. Blue opal can also be an antidote to restless thoughts that keep one awake at night. Placing a blue opal in the pillowcase will help one sleep peacefully. Crystal healers say that it helps calm respiratory inflammations and chronic coughs due to asthma. They contend it even helps relieve eczema or psoriasis. Overall, blue as well as other opal strengthens the will to live.

Evaluation and Pricing of Common Opal

Because of their rarity, blue, green and pink are the most valued common opal hues. Translucency, intensity of color, and the freedom from distracting imperfections are the key determinants of high quality. Retail price ranges for these opals are listed in Table 9.1 The information was provided by Jürgen Schütz, president of Emil Weis Opals, a company with an extensive selection of common and precious opals.

Table 9.1 Retail per-carat price ranges of blue, green and pink opal

Opal Color	Retail Range of High Quality	Commercial Quality
Blue	US$ 200–300 / ct	US$ 80–100 / ct
Green	US$ 100–150 / ct	US$ 20–30 / ct
Pink	US$ 50–80 / ct	US$ 10–20 / ct

Blue, green and pink opal that is semiopaque, very porous and highly included sells for much less than the above prices. The lowest price colors of common opal are white, gray and black.

Banded opal, landscape opal and fluorite opal are often sold by the piece or the strand with the prettiest and most unusual patterns fetching the highest prices. Since these stones are so rare and each one is different, it's hard to predict their price. Landscape opal from Peru, however, typically ranges from US$ 2–20 per carat.

Expect to pay more for opal beads and cabochons than for those of quartz and chalcedony, which are plentiful. Availability of the material affects price. When mines close, prices often go up, so prices can vary from one year to another. With the exception of the white, gray and black varieties, most common opal is relatively scarce.

When opals are set in jewelry or carved, other factors enter into their pricing— such as the amount of time required to carve it, the uniqueness of the design and gem material, and the skill and prestige of the designer. It takes talent to turn common opal into an extraordinary jewel.

Fire Opal

The Aztecs of central Mexico were mesmerized by the vivid red and orange colors of fire opal. To them it represented all the virtues of the sun—energy, light, warmth and life itself. Fire opal was used in their rituals and ceremonies and included in their burial sites. The Spaniards under Hernando Cortés were also fascinated with Mexican opals and took them back to Europe during the first quarter of the 16th century. For more than 300 years after the destruction of the Aztec civilization by the Spaniards, the opal mines were closed, and their location remained a closely guarded secret by the native population. In 1855, those mines were rediscovered in Querétaro by a plantation worker at the Hacienda Esperanza, about 150 miles (241 kilometers) northwest of Mexico City. The Querétaro opal deposit eventually became the most important precious fire opal producing area in the world. However, the Magdalena area in the state of Jalisco has become a strong competitor. Opals were discovered there in 1948.

Red and orange opals are not the only types found in Mexico. Some have a base color of white, black or colorless, but they are not fire opals. Mexican opals may be solid opal (entirely opal) or matrix opal (surrounded and/or interspersed within their host rock). Transparent to semitransparent opals that display a play-of-color or none at all and that have a colorless or near-colorless body color are called **water opals**.

Water opals and fire opals come from the same mining locations, but they have different names because fire opals are not colorless. Their body color is red, orange or yellow.

Sometimes Mexican opals show a play-of-color when they are held between a light source and the viewer's eye. Opals that display rainbow colors in transmitted light are called ***contra luz,*** meaning "against the light" in Spanish. Examples of contra luz opals are shown in figures 10.3 & 10.4.

Opals come in a wide variety of choices. Many collectors like to buy one of each type from the various countries in which they are found. If you would like to buy an opal for yourself or as a gift, you can find one in any color and almost any price range.

Why "Fire Opal" is a Confusing Term

The term "fire opal" is confusing because some opal dealers refer to "play-of-color" as "fire," a term used by diamond dealers for the dispersion of white light into spectral colors. Dispersion and play-of-color are two separate optical phenomena. Since "fire" is often used in the trade to also mean play-of-color, some assume that fire opals have play-of-color. However, most fire opals have none. In the previous chapter, I defined fire opal as an opal with a red, orange, yellow or brownish body color, with or without a play-of-color, which is generally how it is defined by gemological organizations.

ig. 10.1 Mexican opals from Emil Weis Opals. Top: fire opal, right: black opal, bottom: water opal, ft: can be called a fire opal or water opal. *Photo by Tanja Schütz.*

Top left: Fig. 10.2 Matrix opal and fire opals from Mexico. *Photo © H. A. Hänni, SSEF Swiss Gemmological Institute.*

Bottom left: Fig. 10.3 Faceted Contra luz fire opals viewed against the light. *Opals from Opalos de México; photo by Juan José Virgen Alatorre.*

Fig. 10.4 Mexican contra luz opal (11.58 cts). *Opal & photo: Coast-to-Coast Rarestones International.*

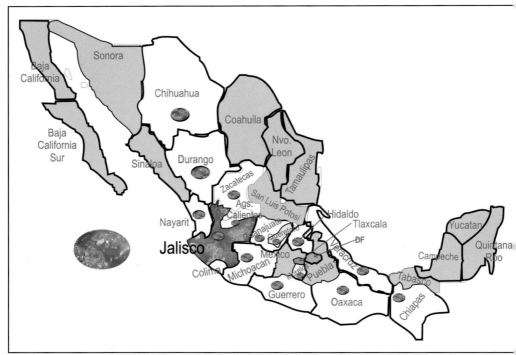

Fig. 10.5 Map of Mexico showing opal mining areas. *Map by Juan José Virgen Alatorre.*

Fig. 10.6 Opal miner in Magdalena, Jalisco in Mexico. *Photo: Juan José Virgen Alatorre.*

Fig. 10.7 Workers at an opal mine in Jalisco, Mexico. *Photo: Juan José Virgen Alatorre.*

Some have proposed calling fire opal, "Mexican opal" since most of it comes from Mexico. However, calling an opal from another country "Mexican opal" would be inaccurate and misleading. In addition, many opals from Mexico do not have an orange, yellow or red body color.

Some fire-opal dealers have found a way to avoid the terminology confusion. Fire has red, orange, and yellow colors, so they call opal with body colors in the red to yellow range fire opal. However, they refer to opal play-of-color as "rain" (*lluvia*) since the play-of-color in opal can have the same spectral colors as those in a rainbow.

Let's look at an example of how Mexican terminology can be applied to the description of an opal. Juan José Virgen Alatorre, an opal specialist, dealer and author of *Magdalena, Famosa Tierra de Ópalos* (*Magdalena, Famous Land of Opals*), describes the uncut opal in figure 10.8 as an orange fire opal with rain colors of green, blue, orange, and yellow. The opal could also be described simply as a precious fire opal, but that would not provide information about the play-of-color hues.

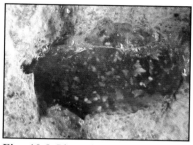

Fig. 10.8 Play-of-color in fire opal from Opalos de México. *Photo by Juan José Virgen Alatorre.*

This chapter will refer to "rain" as play-of-color and all opals with yellow/ orange/red body colors as fire opals. "Rain" colors may be a play of green, blue, red, or whatever other color is present. Since there are various ways to describe and identify opals, it's best to define terminology before identifying and describing these gems.

Geographic Sources of Fire Opal

Most fire opal is from volcanic areas in Mexico containing silica-rich rhyolite and iron, which gives fire opal its orange and red colors. The states of Querétaro, Nayarit and Jalisco are primary sources, but fire opal is found in many other states, too, as the map in figure 10.5 shows.

Fire opal is also mined outside of Mexico. Figures 10.9 & 10.10 show carved opals from Tanzania and Oregon. Examples of fire opal from Brazil are shown in figures 10.11 & 10.12. The Spring 2010 issue of *Gems & Gemology* (pp. 114–121) contains an article about a new occurrence of fire opal without play-of-color from Bemia, Madagascar. The refractive index and specific gravity values of Madagascar fire opal are generally higher than those of other natural fire opals and some synthetic opal. The same issue of *Gems & Gemology* (pp 90–105) also has an article about play-of-color opal from Wengel Tena, Wollo Province, Ethiopia, which includes photos of fire opal.

In addition, small amounts of fire opal have been found in Australia, Honduras, Turkey, Indonesia, Somalia, Kazakhstan, and Canada.

Opal Treatments and Assembled Stones

Various methods have been developed to enhance the appearance of opal, disguise cracks and/or make them more durable. These include:

Fig. 10.9 Fire opal from Oregon carved by Sherris Cottier Shank. *Photo by Amy Balthrop.*

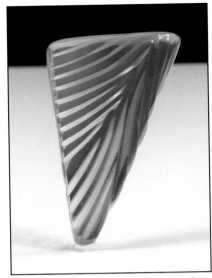

Fig. 10.10 Fire opal from Tanzania carved by Sherris Cottier Shank. *Photo by Amy Balthrop.*

Fig. 10.11 Fire opals from Brazil. *Photo by Wolf Kuehn of the Canadian Institute of Gemmology*

Fig. 10.12 Fire opals from Brazil. *Photo by Wolf Kuehn of the Canadian Institute of Gemmology.*

Fig. 10.13 A "tizate" opal before burning. *Opal from Opalos de México; photo by Juan José Virgen Alatorre.*

Fig. 10.14 A "tizate" opal after treatment. *Opal from Opalos de México; photo by Juan José Virgen Alatorre.*

Impregnation: Some opals have a tendency to crack due to loss of water from the opal structure. Resins, wax, plastic and silicon sealants are used to seal cracks and make the opals more stable. Oil is sometimes used to hide cracks but it does not last. The specific gravity of impregnated opals tends to be less than that of untreated opal. One should avoid repolishing or applying solvents to treated opal.

Burning treatment (*Tizate ópalo quemado*): A very dry, porous natural white opal called "tizate" opal is burned on yellow sand, turning it black (figs. 10.13 & 10.14). This delicate process requires expertise because if the stone is heated too long, it will break or burst. Placing the treated opal in water after treatment can cause the the opal to return to its original state or make it look spotted. The opal cannot be retreated to blacken it. Therefore, avoid exposing "tizate" treated opals to water or liquids after treatment.

Smoke treatment: During smoke treatment, opals are wrapped in paper or sand and then heated. Soot particles penetrate the opal and darken it, making the colors stand out. When moisture is applied to the surface, the opal turns black, but the blackness goes away when the moisture dries. The play-of-color of smoke-treated stones generally looks unnatural and their surface is easily damaged.

Sugar treatment: Porous white opal is sometimes soaked and heated in a sugar solution followed by immersion in concentrated sulphuric acid. The acid reacts chemically with the sugar to produce carbon and create a dark background, which emphasizes the play-of-color. However, the polish tends to be less lustrous than naturally colored black opal, and the play-of-color is often patchy. With the unaided eye, good quality sugar-treated opal can be hard to differentiate from natural black opal. However, under magnification, black carbon particles are visible around particles of gem opal and in the voids of the surrounding matrix. Most sugar-treated opal is mined in Andamooka in South Australia.

Dye (Staining) treatment: Colored dyes are sometimes used on play-of-color opals to darken them; and on common opals, dyes may be used to improve or even out their colors. Under magnification, dye concentrations may be visible.

Opal doublet (Doublet opal): This assembled stone is a thin slice of natural opal cemented usually with black or brown glue to another material such as potch opal, chalcedony, obsidian, glass or boulder matrix (fig. 10.15). Any opal with a flat or gently domed upper surface should be suspected of being a doublet. When unmounted, it is easy to see the junction between the base and the opal. However, it may not be visible if the opal is surrounded by a bezel or mounted in a closed back. Do not confuse doublets with boulder opal, which has a naturally attached backing. Often you can detect man-made doublets by looking at them from the side. A doublet typically has a straight separation line whereas a boulder opal has a crooked one.

Opal triplet (Triplet opal): This is a thin slice of natural opal cemented between a dark base and a colorless quartz or crystal glass top, which protects the opal and magnifies the play-of-color because of its dome shape (fig. 10.16). Triplets are normally less expensive than doublets because less opal is used. The bottom of the opal in doublets and triplets is sometimes backed with foil, paint or mother of pearl in order to improve the color and brilliance of the opal.

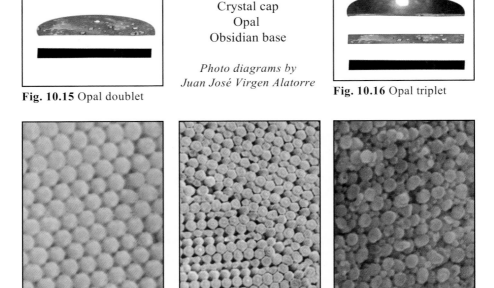

Crystal cap
Opal
Obsidian base

Photo diagrams by
Juan José Virgen Alatorre

Fig. 10.15 Opal doublet

Fig. 10.16 Opal triplet

Figs. 10.17–10.19 Scanning electron micrographs of opals at 40,000x magnification. Left: precious opal, Center: precious opal with a color boundary, Right: potch. *Photos courtesy of Division of Minerals and Energy Resources, Primary Industries and Resources, South Australia.*

Identifying Traits of Natural, Synthetic & Imitation Opal

Opal is a non-crystalline form of silica, $SiO_2 \cdot H_2O$, chemically similar to quartz (SiO_2), but containing usually 3–10% water but sometimes up to 20%. The lower the amount of water, the less likely the opal is to craze (crack) from heat and temperature changes. Opal's basic structure of silicon dioxide is a dense accumulation of minute spheres with a diameter of less than 0.0005 mm. In opals with a play-of-color, the spheres are regularly arranged in a three-dimensional grid and are of equal size throughout (figs. 10.17 & 10.18). The evenly spaced gaps in the grid allows white light to be diffracted into rainbow colors. In common opal with no play-of-color, the spheres are arranged randomly and vary in size (fig. 10.19).

In most cases, it is fairly easy to distinguish play-of-color opal from other gems by its appearance. However, synthetic opal may be mistaken for natural opal. Under magnification, lab-grown opal typically has a hexagonal pattern resembling chicken wire when viewed with overhead or backlighting. From the side it may have a columnar structure. Synthetic opal usually has a lower specific gravity than natural opal because it is often impregnated with plastic substances. Some synthetic opals have a spectrum with bands at 550 nm and 580 nm. Most natural white opal phosphoresces green after exposure to long-wave ultraviolet light, whereas synthetic opal does not. Kyocera, Inamori, and Gilson are three producers of man-made opal.

Synthetic opal without a play-of-color is produced in a variety of colors. Two examples are the orange "MexiFire and blue "PeruBlu" lab-grown opals, which were manufactured

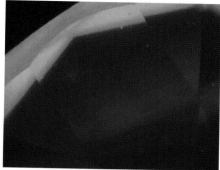

Fig. 10.20 Densely spread minute inclusions and gas bubbles in "Mexifire" lab-grown opal. *Photo: GAAJ-Zenhokyo Laboratory.*

Fig. 10.21 Fine wavy growth structure in "MexiFire" opal. *Photo from the GAAJ-Zenhokyo Laboratory.*

by RMC Gems Thai Co. Ltd. Under magnification, they do not have the characteristic "lizard skin" appearance of synthetic opal, but do have gas bubbles and densely spread minute inclusions that form clouds (fig. 10.20). Their fine wavy growth structure is unlike that of natural opal (fig. 10.21). More information is available on the GAAJ (Gemmological Association of All Japan) website at www.gaaj-zenhokyo.com and in an article entitled "A New Type of Synthetic Fire Opal: Mexifire"in the Fall 2008 issue of *Gems & Gemology* (pp. 228-233).

Fire opal without play-of-color can be confused with other orange gems. Two of the most common fire opal look-alikes are carnelian and spessartine (figs. 10.26 & 10.27). Other materials that may be confused with fire opal are hessonite, coral, citrine, sapphire, topaz, amber and plastic. They can easily be separated from opal by refractive index, specific gravity (SG) and magnification. Some typical fire opal inclusions are shown in figures 10.23–10.25.

Glass and plastic opal imitations are sometimes misrepresented as natural opal. The refractive index of glass and plastic is usually higher than that of opal, and under magnification, they both may show gas bubbles, flow lines and swirls. The low heft (specific gravity) of plastic also helps separate it from natural opal. Slocum Stone is one of the best-known glass imitations of opal. Its opalescence is produced by very thin layers of metallic film in the form of translucent flakes. Opalite, another imitation, is made of layered glass with metal oxide between the layers. Buyers should be aware that the term "opalite" is also used to refer to various forms of chalcedony and common opal. Other glass imitations are occasionally created by adding flecks of colored foil to molten glass. An imitation made of small fragments of real opal set in a black resin has been encountered, too.

Industrial grade opal is sometimes reconstituted (reconstructed), which means it's crushed and mixed with acrylic resins to provide an inexpensive alternative to natural opal. Natural opal in reconstituted matrix is also sold on the market.

Mosaic and chip opals are a composition of small flat or irregularly shaped pieces of natural opal cemented as a mosaic tile on a dark base material or encompassed in a resin.

Opal imitations are not new. Two thousand years ago Pliny the Elder, author of *Naturalis Historia*, wrote, "There is no stone that is imitated by fraudulent dealers with more exactness than [opal], in glass, the only mode of detecting the imposition being by the light of the sun. For when a false opal is held between the finger and thumb, and exposed to the rays of that luminary, it presents but one and the same color throughout, limited to the body of the stone; whereas the genuine opal offers various refulgent rays in succession, and reflects now one hue and now another, as it sheds its luminous brilliancy upon the fingers."

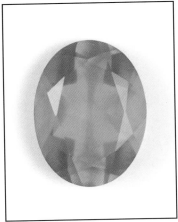

Fig. 10.22 "PeruBlu" lab-grown opal. *Photo courtesy of the GAAJ-Zenhokyo Laboratory.*

Fig. 10.23 Coral-like stalagmite/stalactite formations are clearly seen under magnification of this fire opal from Pala Gems Intl. *Photo by Wimon Manorotkul.*

Fig. 10.24 Macro view of needle-like inclusions in fire opal, which are referred to as *pelos* (hairs) or *pajitos* (little straws) in Spanish. *Photo by Juan José Virgen.*

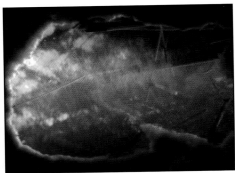

Fig. 10.25 Photomicrograph of inclusions in fire opal. *Photo by Anthony de Goutière.*

Fig. 10.26 Carnelian (chalcedony), which is sometimes confused with fire opal. *Cab and photo from New Era Gems.*

Fig. 10.27 Spessartine, another fire-opal look-alike. *Photo by Bear Williams of Stone Group Laboratories.*

Details about the physical and optical properties of opal are provided below:

Table 10.1

Identifying Characteristics of Opal		
RI: 1.45 (+0.20, -0.80) Mexican opal may be as low as 1.37, but usually 1.42–1.43	SG: 2.15 (+.08, -.9) Many synthetic opals are impregnated with a polymer to make them more stable, and this leads to a lower SG than most natural opal.	
Hardness: 5–6.5	Birefringence: none	Cleavage: none
Toughness: fair–very poor	Crystal System: amorphous; Optic Char: SR, ADR (anomalous double refraction) common due to strain	
Pleochroism: None	Polish luster: Vitreous to resinous	
Fracture: Conchoidal to uneven; Fracture luster: Subvitreous to waxy		
Spectrum: Normally not diagnostic; green opal has cutoffs at 470 nm and 660 nm; some green synthetic opal shows bands at 550 nm and 580 nm; orange to red untreated synthetic opal may show general absorption to 500 nm followed by a band at 550 nm and a line at 580 nm; blue polymer treated synthetic opal may show bands at 540, nm 580 nm and 630 nm; red or pink polymer treated synthetic opal may show a broad absorption band in the green or green-blue, sometimes accompanied by a band around 580 nm or 610 nm.		
Fluorescence: Common opal—inert to strong green or yellowish green (LW and SW); may phosphoresce; black or white opal—inert to white to moderate light blue, green or yellow (LW and SW), may phosphoresce; fire opal—inert to moderate greenish brown (LW and SW); may phosphoresce.		
Crystal habit (form): none, amorphous		
Geological setting: Opal is deposited in cavities and fissures in rocks from low temperature, silica bearing water. Opal may also replace existing structures such as fossils or soluble minerals. In Australia, it forms in sedimentary deposits (marl); in Mexico, in volcanic rocks (rhyolite). It's extracted mainly from primary deposits in open-cast and underground mines.		
Stability: Stable to light; sudden temperature changes may cause opals to crack or craze; over heating will turn most opals white or brownish, and the play-of-color will disappear; attacked by hydrofluoric acid and caustic alkalies.		
Treatments: Impregnation with oil, wax, plastic, or smoke; dyeing with aniline dye, silver nitrate, or sugar carbonized by acid; backing with reflective foil, black paint, etc.		

Most of the above technical data was based on *Gems: Fourth Edition* by Robert Webster, *Color Encyclopedia of Gemstones* by Joel Arem (1987), *GIA Gem Reference Guide,* the GIA *Gem Identification Lab Manual* (2005), the Gem A *Diploma in Gemmology Course* (2009) of the British Gemmological Association, *Handbook of Gem Identification* by Richard T. Liddicoat, and *Dana's Manual of Mineralogy,* 18th Edition, Cornelius Hurlbut.

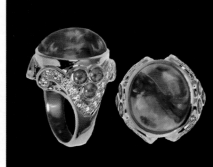

Figs. 10.29–10.33 Fire opal jewelry designed and created by Paula Crevoshay. Fire opal goddess carved by Glenn Lehrer. *Photos by Chris Chavez.*

Fig. 10.34 Fire opal earrings by Zaffiro. *Photo: Daniel Van Rossen.*

Fig. 10.35 Fire opal pendant by Mark Anderson of Different Seasons Jewelry. *Photo: Jessica Dow.*

Fig. 10.36 Opal pendant by Hubert Inc. *Photo by Josian Gattermeier*

Fig. 10.37 Fire opal pendant by Zaffiro. *Photo: Daniel Van Rossen.*

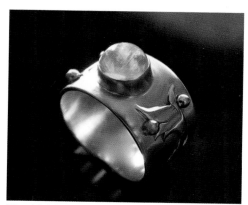

Fig. 10.38 Fire opal bowl pendant from Dancing Designs. *Photo by Tom DeGasperis.*

Fig. 10.39 Fire opal ring by Mark Anderson of Different Seasons Jewelry. *Photo: Jessica Dow.*

Figs. 10.40–10.45 Fire opal jewelry designed and created by Yossi Harari. *Photos from Muse Imports.*

Fig. 10.46 Photo by John Parrish.

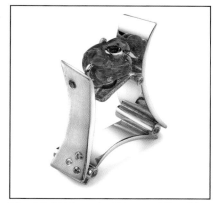

Fig. 10.47 Photo by Diamond Graphics

Fig. 10.48 Photo by Dane Ammon

Fig. 10.49 Photo by Diamond Graphics

Fig. 10.50 Photo by Dane Ammon

Figs. 10.46–10.50 Fire opal jewelry designed and made by Mark Schneider.

Metaphysical Properties of Fire Opal

Fire opal's energy is said to prevent burn-out and be conducive to progress and change. It adds brilliance and clarity to the intuitive process and awakens an inner fire that helps achieve whatever one's heart desires. Used in situations of injustice and mistreatment, fire opal helps people work through emotional turmoil and release deep-seated feelings of grief so they can let go of the past. When fire opal is placed in a room, it is said to reduce hostility and offensive behavior by dissipating negative energy. According to metaphysical specialists, fire opal also:

◆ Calms the nerves and eases depression and apathy

◆ Aids in all disorders of the blood

◆ Stimulates the sexual organs

◆ Disperses gallstones, kidney stones, and calcium deposits

◆ Treats disorders of the central nervous system

◆ Provides insight into the attitudes that cause one's health problems

Pricing & Evaluation of Fire Opal

The price range of fire opals is enormous. They can sell for a $1 a carat or several thousand dollars per carat. Generally speaking, fire opals without play-of-color retail for less than $1000 per carat even in extra fine qualities. If they are of commercial quality, you can find them for under $100 per carat. Low quality stones sell for less than $10 per carat. There is also a wide price variation for opals with play-of-color. The stones that fetch thousands of dollars per carat have a bright play of multiple intense colors throughout the stone, which are visible from every angle as the stone is moved, even on a white piece of paper. These stones are often bought directly by Japanese or German dealers. To help you better understand opal evaluation, price factors are listed below:

Durability, resistance to crazing: This is an important factor in determining value. Some opals, particularly from North and Central America (e.g., Mexican fire opal) are very susceptible to developing fine cracks that resemble a spider's web (crazing), even when they are not subjected to strong heat. These stones generally craze a few days after they are mined and are discarded. Opals with a high water content are the ones most subject to crazing.

Ethical dealers wait a few years before selling their opals and check them carefully to see if they have crazed or become cloudy after exposure to normal atmospheric conditions. Fire opals that withstand polishing and an initial wait period of at least three years without any sign of crazing are likely to resist crazing after they are purchased, Many dealers offer some type of guarantee against crazing that is typically valid for at least a year. However, this guarantee is not against cracks that are the result of abuse or poor setting skills. It is important to avoid storing opals in very hot and dry environments. For example, jewelers and museums should not display opals under hot lights or in a sunny window.

Opals occasionally have pattern lines which look like cracks but aren't. These lines are natural changes in the pattern of an opal and are not regarded as flaws.

Fig. 10.51 Crazed opal. © Renée Newman   **Fig. 10.52** Mexican matrix opal from Opalos de México. *Photo by Juan José Virgen.*

Opal type: Solid Mexican opal is more expensive than matrix opal (opal naturally attached to its host rock) if similar qualities and colors of each category are compared. Assembled stones (doublets and triplets) are the least expensive types. There is a great difference in price between a solid opal and an assembled one of similar appearance, so it is important to have the salesperson identify the type of opal both verbally and on the receipt.

Size and Carat Weight: The price of opals varies according to size, weight and quality. Stones weighing less than a carat are generally worth less per carat than larger ones of the same quality. The price per carat increases as the weight increases. Opals between six and ten carats tend to have the highest per-carat price. If a stone is unusually large, it is worth more per carat than stones more suitable for general jewelry use because there are only a few stones above ten carats every year. Consequently, they are in high demand, especially by opal connoisseurs. Matrix opals are typically priced by the amount of opal visible in the stone. A small stone with a lot of opal can be higher priced than a large one with little opal.

Body tone: (The darkness or lightness of the background color): Medium to medium dark tones are normally more highly valued than light tones. With play-of-color opals that are dark enough to be classified as a black opal, usually the darker the background the more valuable the stone. When determining body tone, look at the top of the stone. Natural Mexican black opal in good quality is very rare and very expensive. The brightness of the play-of-color is more important than the body tone.

Sometimes Mexican opal is heated and smoked in paper to blacken it. Mexican doublets may also look like black opals. It is relatively easy to identify these doublets because of their black obsidian base. The black background makes the play-of-color stand out more. As with all opals, doublets come in various quality grades.

Body color hue: Red, red-orange and orange are generally considered to be the most valuable hues for a fire opal, followed by yellow-orange, yellow and red-brown.

Transparency: The higher the transparency, the more valuable the stone, all other factors being equal.

Imperfections: Opal value decreases when there are eye-visible imperfections on the top of the stone such as white areas or needle-like inclusions. The larger and more noticeable they are, the greater their impact on value. Inclusions on the back of a stone have little or no effect on price unless they hurt the structural integrity of the stone. Cracks drastically reduce value. In fine quality opals, those without any imperfections are priced the highest.

Play-of-color: The intensity and variety of colors are both important. For example, stones whose color play shows all colors of the spectrum are more valued than those with flashes of two colors. The way in which different color combinations are priced can vary from one dealer to another. Any type of play-of-color can be desirable, as long as the colors are intense and not dull when viewed face up. Keep in mind that the color play and body color of the stone are affected by the lighting and position of the stone. Top quality stones show a good play of color from all angles.

Play-of-color pattern: The diffracted colors in opals are displayed in various patterns: **pinfire**—small pinpoint like color specks; **flashfire**—larger splashes of color, usually irregular in shape; **broad flashfire**—sheets of color normally covering a large section or all of a stone's surface; **fancy patterns and picture stones**— unusual patterns that form pictures or resemble things such as Chinese writing, straw, flowers, etc. Pinfire and small type patterns are generally priced lower than broad patterns or large flashes.

Brightness: The brighter and more intense the flashes of color, the better the stone. Examine brightness both under a consistent light source and away from it. Stones that maintain their brilliance away from light are the most highly valued, which is why brightness is one of the most important value factors.

Shape: The most sought-after traditional cabochon shape for opals with play-of-color is a well-formed oval. It tends to bring a higher price than other shapes because it's in greater demand, it's easier to set, and valuable opal material is sacrificed when stones are cut as ovals. Many jewelers and designers, however, prefer other shapes, especially freeforms because they are more distinctive (figs. 10.53 & 10.54), particularly after they are mounted.

Cut: All else being equal, domed cabochons tend to be more valued than flat ones. Excessive weight on the bottom and a thin or asymmetrical profile can all reduce the value of an opal. Fire opals with no play-of-color are normally faceted. Cut quality affects their price in the same way it does other faceted colored gems in that faceting should maximize the color and brilliance of the stone. If an opal has been carved, the workmanship and skill of the carver should be considered.

Keep in mind that every opal is unique. Cutters must let the characteristics of each opal guide them in order to choose the cut that will maximize its beauty.

Treatment status: Untreated opals are more highly valued than those that are treated with dyes, smoke, epoxies, and other substances used to improve appearance and stability.

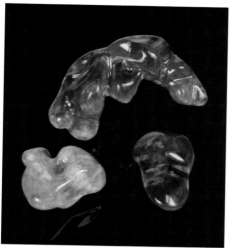

Fig. 10.53 Fire opal freeforms from Hubert Inc. *Photo by Josian Gattermeier.*

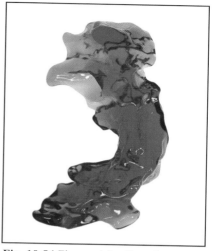

Fig. 10.54 Fire opal freeform from Emil Weis Opals. *Photo by Tanja Schütz.*

Fig. 10.55 Fire opal carving by Meg Berry from New Era Gems. *Photo © R. Newman.*

Fig. 10.56 Same carving as in figure 10.55 from a different angle. *Photo © R. Newman.*

Opal evaluation is a challenge because there are many price factors and many different types of opals. Two thousand years ago Pliny the Elder, author of *Naturalis Historia*, wrote, "Of all precious stones, it is opal that presents the greatest difficulty of description. It displays at once the piercing fire of carbunculus [garnet], the purple brilliance of amethystos, and the sea green of smaragdus [emerald], the whole blended together with a brightness that is incredible."

The diversity of opal is a positive feature because it offers buyers a wide range of choices and designers the opportunity to create pieces that cannot be replicated. After viewing the stones and jewelry images in this chapter, I hope you will have a greater appreciation for the beauty of fire opals.

Caring for Opal

Clean opals using a soft cloth, a mild soap and room temperature water. Then rinse to remove any residue. Clean doublets and triplets with the same method, but don't soak them. Soaking can dissolve the glue holding the layers together. Do not use steam cleaners or ultrasonics to clean opals; the heat could make them crack and cleaning solutions in ultrasonics would be absorbed because opals are porous. Avoid chemicals and activities that could cause abrasions, pressure or knocks. Opals should not come in contact with a jeweler's torch.

Keep in mind that opals contain water. This makes them especially sensitive to sudden temperature changes and hot, dry weather conditions. If opals are placed in a sunny display window, under hot lights, near a heat source or worn while sunbathing, they may crack or craze (develop tiny fissures like the glaze of pottery).

If you've attended a mineral show, you may have noticed that some dealers store opals in water. This helps to accentuate the play-of-color while keeping them moist. It's not necessary to store opals in water, but when opals are stored in dehumidified or unusually dry environments, it is helpful to store them with a dish of distilled water nearby or in a tight plastic bag. With proper care, opals can give you a lifetime of enjoyment.

11

The Garnet Group

When given as a gift, the garnet is said to bring love and loyalty. According to legend, adorning yourself with garnets will improve your personal relationships and protect you from harm. These benefits are doubled if your birthday is in January, since garnet is the birthstone for January. It's also the second and sixth wedding anniversary stone, the state mineral of Connecticut and the state gem of New York. Grossular, a garnet species, is the state gem of Vermont, and star garnet is the state gem of Idaho.

The name "garnet" comes from the Latin *granatum* meaning pomegranate and grain or seed. In the 13th century, the German theologian and philosopher Albertus Magnus proposed the name garnet to mineralogists because garnet crystals in rock and garnet clusters in jewelry resembled the shape and color of pomegranate seeds. Garnet and other red stones had previously been known as "carbuncles" because of their likeness to small, red-hot coals. For example, in the Bible, one of the twelve stones in the high priest's breastplate was a carbuncle (Exodus 28:17), which is presumed to be a garnet. Today "carbuncle" sometimes refers to a red garnet that is cabochon shaped like a dome with a flat bottom.

Garnet has a long and rich history. Garnet jewelry dating back to 3100 B.C. has been found in the Czech Republic and Egypt. In the fourth and third century B.C., garnet was a favorite stone in Greece and remained popular through Roman times. Besides being used for adornment, garnets were prescribed for heart problems and carved for signet rings to stamp the wax that secured official documents. Ancient surgeons put garnet on wounds to stop bleeding. Warriors carried garnet to protect themselves from death and injury and to bring victory and peace. Even today, some soldiers in the Middle East and Asia wear garnet as a protective talisman. In India, garnet jewelry was often buried with the dead to light their way into the next life. Native American Indians used garnets in their ornaments.

Red garnets were the basis for a thriving jewelry and cutting center in Bohemia, Czech Republic, which started in around 1500. Bohemia remained the world's major source of garnet until the late nineteenth century; in fact Bohemian garnets were widely used in Victorian jewelry throughout the 1800's. Figures 11.1–11.3 show three examples. Russian demantoid garnet was also popular during Victorian times. See Chapter 12.

Garnet is a group of related mineral species, six of which are used as gems— andradite, pyrope, almandine, spessartine, grossular and uvarovite. Garnets are found in all colors including orange, yellow, green, blue, violet, brown, black and colorless as well as the more traditional maroon, red and purple colors. Garnet gems are normally a mixture of more than one species, with one or two members predominating. The relationships among these members are shown in figures 11.5 and 11.6. Trade names are included in figure 11.6. Varieties within each series are differentiated by their own specific colors.

Fig. 11.1 Bohemian garnet locket/pin/pendant from Lang Antique & Estate Jewelry. *Photo by Thomas Picarella.*

Fig. 11.2 Bohemian garnet brooch (circa 1880's) from Lang Antique & Estate Jewelry. *Photo by Thomas Picarella.*

Fig. 11.3 Bohemian garnet bangle bracelet from Lang Antique & Estate Jewelry. *Photo by Thomas Picarella.*

Fig. 11.4 Garnet suite. © *H. A. Hänni, SSEF Swiss Gemmological Institute.*

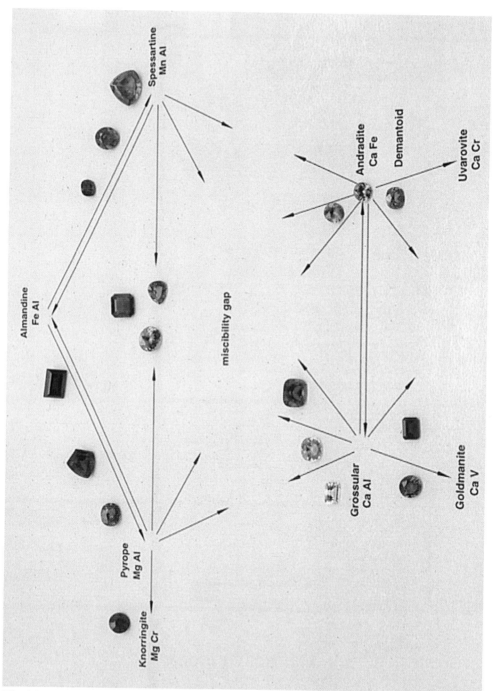

Fig. 11.5 Garnet diagram showing upper Pyralspites, lower Ugrandites. Hypothetic members are knorringite and goldmanite, who are giving color as admixtures in solid solution. © *H. A. Hänni, SSEF Swiss Gemmological Institute.*

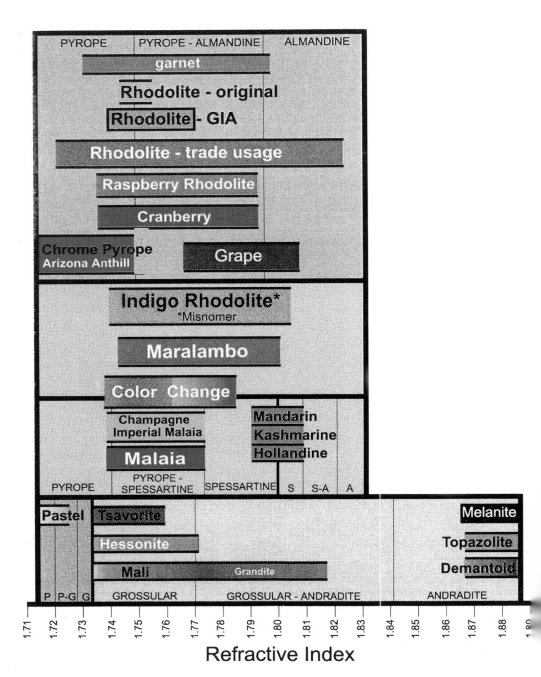

Fig. 11.6 Garnet classification chart from *Naming Gem Garnets* by W. Wm. Hanneman, PhD. © *1999 W. W. Hanneman.*

Table 11.1 Gem Garnets and Their Refractive Index Values (RIs)

Species, end member	Varieties & trade names	Basic Color	RI GIA	RI Hanneman
Andradite	Demantoid Topazolite Melanite Rainbow garnet	Green Yellow or orange Black Iridescent	1.888	1.841–1.887
Uvarovite	Uvarovite	Green	1.798–1.864	–
Spessartine*	Kashmirine Hollandine Mandarin garnet	Orange Orange Orange	1.79–1.814	1.774–1.809
Almandine*		Purple	1.78–OTL**	1.795–1.830
Grossular-andradite	Grandite or Mali garnet	Yellow-green Yellow-green, brown	1.762–1.779	1.770–1.841
Pyrope-spessartine	Color change Malaya garnet Blue garnet Imperial garnet Champagne garnet	Variable Red-orange, pink-orange Blue Red-orange, pink-orange Pinkish brown	1.75–1.78	1.740–1.774
Pyrope-almandine	Rhodolite Grape garnet	Purple-red or pink Purple	1.75–1.78	1.749–1.795
Pyrope	Pyrope Chrome pyrope Anthill garnet Gypsy rose	Red to brownish red Red Red Orange-red	1.73–1.75	1.714–1.749
Grossular*	Grossular Hessonite Tsavorite Mint Garnet Imperial garnet	Green, yellow, brown colorless, orange Orange, yellow, brown Green Light bluish green Pink, orangish pink	1.73–1.76	1.728–1.770
Hydrogrossular (also called grossular)	Translucent green Translucent white Translucent pink	Green White Pink	1.72 (spot)	

The refractive index values in the above table are from the *GIA Gem Identification Lab Manual* (2005) and the William Hanneman table on page 199 of the 6th edition of Robert Webster's *Gems*.

* The GIA Colored Stones Course uses the terms almandite, spessartite, and grossularite, but Gem A (British Gemmological Association) and mineralogy texts refer to these garnets as almandine, spessartine and grossular, which are the names this book has adopted.

** OTL means over the limits of what a standard refractometer can measure.

Garnet Chemistry

The general formula for the chemical composition of a garnet is $X_3Y_2(SiO_4)_3$, where "X" may be calcium (Ca), magnesium (Mg), iron (Fe) or manganese (Mn) and "Y" may be aluminum (Al), iron (Fe), chromium (Cr) or vanadium (V).

Mineralogists divide the six gem garnet members into two series. One has been called the "pyralspite" series from the names *pyrope*, *almandine* and *spessartine*; the other, the "ugrandite" series from *uvarovite*, *grossular*, and *andradite*. The chemical compositions of each series member is given in Table 11.2

Table 11.2

Pyralspite Series: $X_3Al_2(SiO_4)_3$		Ugrandite Series: $Ca_3Y_2(SiO_4)_3$	
Pyrope	$Mg_3Al_2(SiO_4)_3$	Andradite	$Ca_3Fe_2(SiO_4)_3$
Almandine	$Fe_3Al_2(SiO_4)_3$	Grossular	$Ca_3Al_2(SiO_4)_3$
Spessartine	$Mn_3Al_2(SiO_4)_3$	Uvarovite	$Ca_3Cr_2(SiO_4)_3$

As mentioned before, garnets are normally a combination of more than one species, which creates the wide variation of garnet colors. For example, the blue garnet in figure 11.7 is composed of 39.30% pyrope, 39.50% spessartine, 13.80% grossular, 4.9% goldmanite, 1.4% almandine, and 1.10 % uvarovite. Goldmanite is a rare garnet species not normally used in jewelry. The stone can be simply classified as pyrope-spessartine (the two dominant components), and it is in the same category as most color-change garnets, some of which display a blue color in daylight. This blue garnet from Henry A. Hänni is unique because it remains blue both in daylight and under incandescent lighting.

Fig. 11.7 Blue pyrope-spessartine, 0.66 ct, 5.82 mm from Bekily, Madagasgcar. *Photo © H. A. Hänni, SSEF Swiss Gemmological Institute.*

Naming Gem Garnets

Numerous trade names are included in figure 11.6 and Table 11.1. Some names such as kashmirine (or kashmarine) and Mali garnet originated from the areas in which the garnets were found. Other names were created by trade members to make it easier to market the gems and/or to differentiate them from other stones in the same category.

Figure 11.8 is an example of an orange-red garnet from Tanzania with a trade name, "gypsy rose garnet." John Dyer, who cut the stone, had some samples of the Tanzanian rough analyzed by the GIA gem lab because they were different from other red garnets he had cut.

The GIA findings indicated the material had the following characteristics:

Components: 71.1–73.1% pyrope, 18.9–21.7% almandine, 7.0–8.5% grossular, and 0.2–0.4% spessartine, along with traces of the andradite component

Color—Orange-Red;   RI—1.742;   hydrostatic SG—3.8

Absorption lines at 504, 520, and 573 with the desk-model spectroscope

The GIA Laboratory identified the material as pyrope-almandine.

I asked William Hanneman, author of *Naming Gem Garnets*, what he would call a garnet with the preceding characteristics. He said it was pyrope because it was over 70% pyrope. He defines a garnet species (relative to naming gem garnets) as being a gem which is 70% or more of one of the end members. If <70% and >30%, he considers it a mixed species, e.g., pyrope-almandine. Mineralogists determine the species name by the dominant component. If there are only two, then the one that is 51% or more gets the name. If there are more than two then the one that is dominant gets the name.

Fig. 11.8 Gypsy rose garnet (2.87 cts) cut by John Dyer. *Photo by Lydia Dyer.*

I also asked Scottish gemologist Alan Hodgkinson, who has done extensive research on garnets, how he would identify a stone with the above data. His reply was: "To the mineralogist or the gemmologist, the answer is pyrope. However you should appreciate that these two 'camps' approach the identity question from two ends. The mineralogist from the chemistry end, and the gemmologist from the Colour, RI, Spectrum via the spectroscope, and SG end. Either way this gem is a pyrope. However, you will see from what I have mentioned above that with some gems, the two camps will come up with a different answer."

Even among gemologists, opinions differ as to where to draw the line between one garnet species or variety and another, as this gypsy rose garnet example indicates. Two respected garnet researchers state the material is definitely pyrope. A respected gemological lab says it is definitely pyrope-almandine.

Before sending his Tanzanian garnet rough to the GIA for analysis, Dyer asked an appraiser to identify it. The appraiser said it was pyrope-spessartine, which was a reasonable answer, considering that normally, appraisers don't have equipment that will determine the exact chemistry of a garnet. The orange-red color suggests the material might be pyrope-spessartine. Pyrope tends to be reddish, and spessartine is orange. A combination of the two garnet molecules along with those of almandine, which are typically present, could create the orange-red color of the stone. The 3.8 specific gravity falls within the range of a pyrope-spessartine. The RI of 1.742 is a pyrope-range RI, but it is only slightly lower than the 1.75–1.78 range of pyrope-spessartine, which coincidently is the same as that of pyrope-almandine. The absorption lines at 504, 520 and 573 indicate the presence of almandine, but the almandine molecule can also be present in pyrope-spessartine because it is not purely pyrope and spessartine. In addition, the material did not have inclusions indicative of pyrope-almandine. In other words, without doing a chemical analysis of a garnet, it is difficult to predict its exact composition. However, with basic gemological equipment, you can determine that a red stone is a garnet, rather than say a ruby, spinel, or glass.

Garnet dealers and cutters are faced with a real dilemma when selling their stones. Besides the fact that gemologists and mineralogists disagree on how to define garnet species and varieties, the names they assign may not accurately portray the appearance of a gem. For instance, the majority of pyrope-almandines are called rhodolites, which are generally considered to be purplish-red garnets. If Dyer were to call his gypsy-rose garnets either pyrope-almandines or rhodolites, buyers would probably assume his stones were purple-red instead of orange-red. The name "pyrope" also poses problems because many people in the trade visualize pyrope as a dark brownish red stone, with the exception of chrome pyrope which is considered to be only red. If dealers called chrome pyrope, simply pyrope, it would be difficult to sell, so they refer to it as either chrome pyrope or anthill garnet because it is often found in anthills.

John Dyer thought that his rough merited a different name than pyrope or pyrope-almandine because it was brighter and a purer color than common pyrope and a different hue than that of most pyrope-almandine. It resembled the color of a flower variety called "gypsy rose," so he sells stones cut from that type of rough as "gypsy rose garnets." If an appraisal were made of the stone, a species name would be given and the stone's hue, tone and color saturation would be described separately along with comments about the clarity, transparency, faceting style, cut quality, brilliance and carat weight. This information would distinguish it from the traditional images of a pyrope or pyrope-almandine.

When buying garnets, instead of selecting them on the basis of their gemological name, the best approach is to judge them by their appearance and choose those that you consider attractive.

Identifying Garnets

Garnets are singly refractive and have no pleochroism, unlike many gemstones with similar colors and refractive indices such as ruby, sapphire, zircon and chrysoberyl. In addition, garnets have distinctive spectra and internal characteristics that help distinguish them from other gems. Typical inclusions such as the horsetail inclusion in figure 11.9 are discussed in the chapters on the various garnets, which follow this one. Tables 11.3 and 11.4 provide the numerical data you will need to help identify garnets.

Most man-made garnet has been used for lasers and optical equipment or to imitate diamond rather than garnet. However, in recent years, some has been sold as a simulant of demantoid or tsavorite. Although they are called garnets, they really are not because they are not silicates. The first man-made garnet was yttrium aluminum garnet (YAG), which was created in the late 1950's and early 1960's by various labs such as Bell and Linde. YAG has a garnet structure but a different chemical composition than any known natural garnet, so it is considered an imitation.

Fig. 11.9 Horsetail inclusion, *Demantoid: Pala Gems International; photo: Jason Stephenson.*

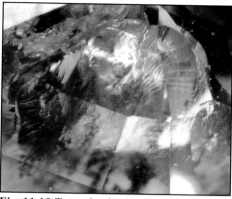

Fig. 11.10 Tsavorite dyed by a new high-tech infusion process that often involves heat and sometimes radiation. *Photo by Robert James of the International School of Gemology*

The RI of YAG is 1.833; SG, 4.5–4.6; and under magnification it may show gas bubbles and sometimes a blue to violet pavilion flash over most facets.

Gadolinium gallium garnet (GGG) was first synthesized in the early 1970's at Bell Laboratories in New Jersey. Like YAG, It has a garnet structure but a different chemical composition than any known natural garnet. Its RI is 1.97; SG, 7.05; and it has a moderate to strong pinkish orange fluorescence under SW, which distinguishes it from natural garnet.

Part of the identification process involves detecting treatments. One of the advantages of garnet is that most of it is untreated and its colors are natural. One exception is demantoid. Some demantoid can undergo a low-temperature heat treatment to lighten or intensify its color, which is stable afterwards. Attempts have been made to improve the appearance of other garnets with heating and diffusion treatment. The October 2004 issue of *The Journal of Gemmology* (pp 205–214) contained an article entitled "A treatment study of Brazilian garnets." Heating and diffusion experiments were performed on Brazilian garnet samples. Most of the heated samples showed no change; however, heating was able to turn light yellow grossular to an Imperial topaz color. Diffusion treatment turned some light yellow grossular green and orange.

Figure 11.10 shows an example of a tsavorite that was dyed by a new high-tech infusion process that often involves heat and sometimes radiation. Color concentrations are visible under magnification. When appraising and identifying garnets, be aware that a few of them might be enhanced, and look for signs of color and clarity enhancement.

The optical and physical properties of garnet are summarized in Tables 11.3 & 11.4. If you would like information on how to use magnetism to distinguish the various garnets, a good resource would be the article entitled "Magnetic susceptibility, a better approach to defining garnets" in the 2008 *Journal of Gemmology* (Nos. 3/4).

Table 11.3

Identifying Characteristics of Garnet		
RI: 1.70–1.89	**SG**: 3.3–4.33	**Dispersion**: 0.022–0.057
Hardness: 6.5–7.5	**Cleavage**: None, but may have indistinct parting	
Toughness: Fair–good	**Pleochroism**: None	
Fracture: Conchoidal	**Polish luster**: Vitreous	**Fracture luster**: greasy to vitreous
Crystal System: Cubic (isometric) **Optic Char**: Singly refractive, anomalous double refraction; AGG for hydrogrossular		
Spectra: See Table 11.4		
Crystal habit (form): Dodecahedron or trapezohedron often in combination, and occasionally hexoctahedron; sometimes in sandy aggregates of fine grains or in massive white, pink or green veins (grossular)		
Geological setting: Pyrope, in igneous rocks; almandine, in metamorphic rocks; spessartine, in pegmatites, rhyolite pockets, and metamorphic rocks with manganese; grossular, metamorphosed limestones; andradite, igneous and metamorphic rocks; uvarovite, metamorphosed chromite deposits.		
Fluorescence: Inert except for some grossular. Near colorless to light green grossular is inert to weak orange under LW and weak yellow-orange under SW.		
Treatments: Usually none, but fracture filling may be done on stones with surface reaching fractures. Some demantoid or other garnets may be heated. Diffusion treatment is possible on some material.		
Stability: Stable to light; sudden temperature changes can make garnet fracture; slightly attacked by hydrofluoric acid.		

Most of the technical data in the above table was based on *Gems: Fourth Edition* by Robert Webster, *GIA Gem Reference Guide*, the GIA *Gem Identification Lab Manual* (2005), the Gem A *Diploma in Gemmology Course* (2009), *Handbook of Gem Identification* by Richard T. Liddicoat, *Rocks and Minerals* by Frederick H. Pough, *Naming Gem Garnets* by William Hanneman, and *Dana's Manual of Mineralogy, 18th Edition*, Cornelius Hurlbut.

Table 11.4 Specific Gravity, Hardness & Spectra Values for Garnets

Species, end member	S.G.	Mohs Hardness	Spectra
Andradite (demantoid)	3.8–3.9	6.5–7	A dark band at 443 nm in yellowish green stones; in rich green stones, a cutoff below 443 nm with fine lines at 620 nm, 632 nm, 693 nm and 700 nm.
Uvarovite	3.71–3.81	7–7.5	Not diagnostic
Spessartine	4.1–4.2	7–7.5	Iron related bands at 505 nm, 527 nm, and 575 nm. Manganese related bands at 412 nm, 424 nm, and 432nm, which sometimes merge to form a cutoff at 430 nm.
Almandine	3.8–4.25	7.25–7.5	Three strong bands in the green and yellow at 505 nm, 527 nm, and 575 nm.
Pyrope-spessartine	3.78–3.85	7–7.5	Strong bands at 410 nm, 420 nm & 430 nm, which sometimes merge to form a cutoff at 435nm. Lines often in the blue to green and yellow at 460 nm, 380nm, 504 nm, 520 nm and 573 nm.
Pyrope-almandine	3.7–3.95	7–7.5	Same as almandine with three strong bands in the green and yellow of the spectrum at 505, 527 nm and 575 nm.
Pyrope	3.7–3.8	7–7.5	505 nm band and a cutoff around 490; chrome pyrope has a band at 505 nm and a broad absorption between 520 and 620 nm; maybe fine lines in the red at 685 nm and 687 nm; cutoff around 490 nm.
Grossular-andradite	3.64–3.68	6.75–7	Similar to yellow andradite's spectrum with a band or cutoff at 440 nm. Intense green stones may show faint lines around 600 nm. Yellowish gre65555en stones may show a weak band at 415 nm, a 440 nm band and faint lines at 465 nm and 495 nm.
Grossular	3.4–3.8	6.75–7.25	Not diagnostic
Hydrogrossular	3.3–3.6	6.75–7.25	Dark green material often shows a cutoff below 460 nm.

Most of the data in the above table was based on *Gems: Fourth Edition* by Robert Webster, *GIA Gem Reference Guide*, the GIA *Gem Identification Lab Manual* (2005), the Gem A *Diploma in Gemmology Course* (2009) of the British Gemmological Association, and the *Handbook of Gem Identification, Twelfth Edition* by Richard T. Liddicoat.

How a Master Cutter Cuts a Garnet

Photos and Captions by Clay Zava
of Zava Mastercuts

Fig. 11.11 Examining the almandine rough for clarity and possible gem shape

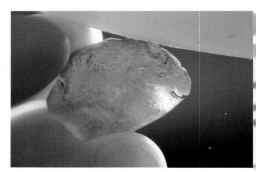

Fig. 11.12 Examining the rough

Fig. 11.13 Cutting a window to see inside the gem

Fig. 11.14 Looking through the gem via the window to determine clarity

Fig. 11.15 Examining the gem to determine potential shapes for cutting

Fig. 11.16 Measuring the gem and assessing the possible shapes for cutting

How a Master Cutter Cuts a Garnet (continued)
Photos and Captions by Clay Zava

Fig. 11.17 Measuring the size of cutoff. This piece will be saved and cut at a later time.

Fig. 11.18 Preparing to saw along a natural crease in the gem

Fig. 11.19 Sawing the gem

Fig. 11.20 The remaining large piece will be preformed, then prepared for cutting

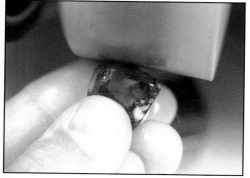

Fig. 11.21

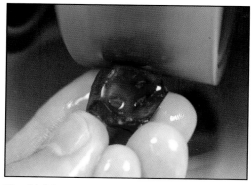

Fig. 11.22

How a Master Cutter Cuts a Garnet (continued)
Photos and Captions by Clay Zava

Fig. 11.23

Fig. 11.25 Examining the final preform

Fig. 11.27 Preform secured to dopstick, ready for cutting

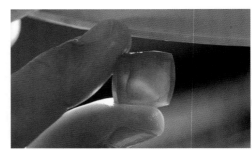

Fig. 11.24 Examining the final preform

Fig. 11.26 A brass dopstick of appropriate size is chosen to secure the preform for cutting.

Fig. 11.28 After the bottom of the pavilion is cut, the gem is transferred to another dopstick of corresponding size for the cutting of the top, or crown.

How a Master Cutter Cuts a Garnet (continued)
Photos and Captions by Clay Zava

Fig. 11.29 The original dopstick is then removed.

Fig. 11.30 A challenge often encountered in cutting is eliminating inclusions during the cutting process

Fig. 11.31 Most inclusions are removed during preforming, but if your estimations are correct, some can be left for more precise removal during cutting.

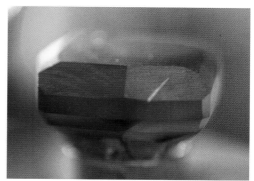

Fig. 11.32 Going

Fig. 11.33 Going

Fig. 11.34 Inclusion gone

How a Master Cutter Cuts a Garnet (continued)
Photos and Captions by Clay Zava

Fig. 11.35 Garnet after the crown is cut

Fig. 11.36 And polished

Fig. 11.37

Fig. 11.38 The top or table facet is the last to be cut.

Fig. 11.39 Close-up view of cutting of table facet

Fig. 11.40 A finished gem almandine. *Photo by John Parrish.*

A Word from a Master Cutter about Garnet

(Text by Clay Zava)

Garnet is a generally straightforward gem to cut. It is durable, singly refractive, and takes a beautiful polish. Although inclusions in garnet are regularly easy to spot and remove during cutting, some of the darker varieties, especially from East Africa, will often have silky inclusions throughout the body of the material that cannot be seen in the rough. To be able to see them, one must cut a "window" or a polished flat place on the gem to know if the material is clear of these minute inclusions. The garnet in figures 11.11–11.40, an Umba garnet, is an example of this.

Another factor that relates to the cutting of garnets is the type of geological deposit in which they're found. The alluvial, or water-worn deposits, of malaya, rhodolite or spessartine garnets will contain solid, rounded off crystals with a frosted surface. In contrast, the mint green garnets of Merelani are often broken off from their host rock, and will contain glassy feathers and fractures from this damage. However, the crystal surfaces of the Merelani mint garnets are clear and easy to see into. Tsavorite garnet rough is often angular and fractured - suggestive of the surface and *in situ* environment it comes from. The high price of tsavorite, coupled with the irregular shape of the rough, creates a particularly daunting task for cutters. The result is often windowed and asymmetrical cuts on commercial goods, and low yields on finely cut gems.

In a word, garnet is particularly rewarding to cut. When time is taken to create a gem with symmetry, order, and a fine polish, the effects are especially beautiful on garnet.

Uvarovite

Even though the garnet uvarovite is not important enough to discuss in a separate chapter, it is sometimes used in jewelry, so I've included it here in this chapter. Since its crystals tend to be too small to facet, uvarovite is normally sold as a cluster of tiny tightly packed crystals called drusy or druse (figs. 11.41 & 11.43). Uvarovite, which ranges in color from green to yellow-green to brownish green was discovered in 1832 by Germain Henri Hess. He named it after Count Sergey Semeonovich Uvarov, a 19th century Russian statesman and scholar. The green color is the result of chromium in the molecular structure of the crystals.

Most uvarovite is found in the Ural Mountains of Russia. Finland, South Africa Quebec and California are secondary sources, but little of this material rivals the beauty of Russian uvarovite. However, some of the Finnish deposits do produce large individual or crystal clusters that are appreciated by mineral collectors.

Uvarovite is usually priced by the piece rather than by carat weight. The best quality specimens have uniform surface coverage of crystals with no exposed matrix. Besides being sold as drusy cabochons and freeforms, uvarovite is also sold on its host rock as a mineral specimen to collectors (fig.11.42).

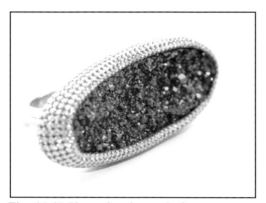 

Fig. 11.41 Uvarovite ring and photo courtesy Anatoly Novik of Elejone Private Collection.

Fig. 11.42 Uvarovite specimen and photo from New Era Gems.

Fig. 11.43 Uvarovite earrings and photo courtesy Anatoly Novik of Elejone Private Collection.

Caring for Garnets

The safest way to clean garnets is to wash them with a mild soap and a soft cloth or brush. Ultrasonics are usually safe but they are risky if liquid inclusions are present. Avoid steam cleaning or exposure to a jeweler's torch because garnets don't tolerate sudden temperature changes. Retipping or repairs on stone settings should be done after the garnet has been removed. When jewelry is sized, garnets should be placed in a water bath or covered it with a heat-shielding product.

Garnets are durable and suitable for daily wear, but if worn in rings on a daily basis, they may become abraded over time and need re polishing. Because of its lower hardness, (usually 6.5) demantoid is less resistant to wear than other garnets. Avoid jumbling garnet jewelry and stones together so as to prevent scratching and abrasions.

It's advisable to have garnet jewelry cleaned and checked by a professional. Many jewelry stores will do this free of charge. With proper care, garnets will remain attractive and offer a lifetime of wear.

Demantoid and Other Andradites

Discovered in the mid 19th century in the Russian Ural Mountains, demantoid was first assumed to be emerald, and was even called Uralian emerald due to its green color. After Finnish mineralogist Nils von Nordenskiöld examined it, he declared it a new mineral. Because of its diamond-like brilliance and fire, he proposed naming it "demantoid," which comes from the Old German *diamant*, or Dutch *demant*, meaning diamond.

It didn't take long for demantoid to become one of the most popular stones of the Victorian and later Edwardian Era. Peter Carl Fabergé and George Kunz of Tiffany's were among its promoters. Nature motifs such as reptiles, birds and flowers were in vogue during the late 19th century, making green demantoids ideal jewelry accents. Sometimes the stones were simply used to frame a piece or surround a center stone. Examples are shown in figures 12.1 – 12.7. Note how most of the stones are melee size. Demantoids above two carats are rare. Sizes below one-half carat are typical.

Fig. 12.1 Russian demantoids encircling a diamond in a Victorian ring from Lang Antique & Estate Jewelry. *Photo by Thomas Picarella.*

Demantoid is a green to greenish yellow variety of andradite, a garnet species named for José Bonifácico de Andrada e Silva, a Brazilian geologist. Traces of chromium are responsible for its green color.

Basic andradite data:
Chemical composition: $Ca_3Fe_2(SiO_4)_3$ — calcium iron silicate
RI: 1.87–1.89, SG: 3.8–3.9, Hardness: 6.5–7.0, Dispersion: 0.057

Geographic Sources of Demantoid

During the 19th century, the Nizhniy Tagil and Sissertsk Russian districts in the Ural mountains were the only sources of demantoid. After the Bolshevik Revolution, gems went out of style in Russia, and minerals were mined primarily for their industrial applications. In the late 1990's, independent Russian miners began to recover notable quantities again. Namibia also became a producer. Consequently, demantoids reemerged on the market. Today, Madagascar is a new significant source. Demantoids have also been found in Italy, Sri Lanka, Iran-Afghanistan border area, California and Quebec.

Jewelry Eras Starting from the 18ᵗʰ Century

Georgian	1714–1837 (reigns of King George I – King George IV)
Victorian	1837–1901 (Queen Victoria 1837–1901)
Arts & Crafts:	1890–1914
Art Nouveau:	1890–1910
Edwardian:	1890–1915 (King Edward VII, 1901–1910) (Belle Epoque)
Art Deco:	1915–1935
Retro:	1935–1955

Antique Demantoid Jewelry

Fig. 12.2 Victorian demantoid and ivory brooch. Skinner auction 9-15-2009, $1,126.00.

Fig. 12.3 Victorian demantoid brooch. Skinner auction 9-16-2008, $652.00.

Fig. 12.4 Edwardian demantoid brooch, Skinner auction 3-16-2010, $1,659.00.

  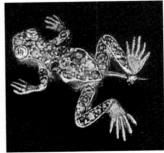

Fig. 12.5 Victorian demantoid brooch, Susanin's auction 12-8-2003, $3,600.

Fig. 12.6 Victorian demantoid ring. Sotheyby's NY auction 12-6-2000, $18,000.

Fig. 12.7 Art Nouveau demantoid brooch. Sotheyby's NY auction 10-20-1999, $4600.

Figs. 12.2–12.7 Photos of antique demantoid jewelry from Gail Brett Levine's www.AuctionMarketResource.com, a comprehensive resource for antique to contemporary gems and jewelry auction sales data. On this website you can view thousands of items sold at jewelry auctions around the world and obtain gallery information, final prices, descriptions and gemological details of the pieces. The prices indicated are hammer prices, which include the buyer's premium.

Fig. 12.8 Demantoids from the Ural Mountains in Russia. The cut stones are over 4 carats each. *Rough and faceted demantoid from Pala Gems; photo by Jeff Scovil.*

Fig. 12.9 From left to right: Russian demantoid, Namibian demantoid, and two topazolites from China. © *H. A. Hänni, SSEF Swiss Gemmological Institute.*

Fig. 12.10 Victorian demantoid & pearl brooch, Skinner auction 12-8-2009, $948.00.

Fig. 12.11 Edwardian demantoid ring. Christie's NY auction 4-9-2002, $99,500.00.

Fig. 12.12 Victorian demantoid brooch. Skinner auction 3-16-10, $2,844.

Figs. 12.10–12.12 Photos of antique demantoid jewelry from Gail Brett Levine's www.AuctionMarketResource.com. Prices indicated are hammer prices with the premium.

Pricing and Evaluation of Demantoid

Demantoid is the most expensive garnet. In sizes above ten carats, extra-fine demantoids have *wholesaled* for more than $20,000 per carat. High quality stones between 2–10 carats can retail for the same amount. Even small stones under a half carat are expensive, with top quality stones retailing for as much as $1200 per carat. Expect to pay about $100–$200 per carat retail for commercial quality half carat stones and $400–$1000 for commercial quality demantoid in the one to two-carat range. Top quality one-carat demantoids can retail for up to $6000.

Color is a key determinant of price. Chromium is responsible for demantoid's green color; without it, andradite's basic colors are yellow and brown. Heating is sometimes done to improve the color of demantoid. Very light or overly dark stones sell for less than demantoids with a medium tone. However, some prefer lighter tones because the dispersion (fire) is more noticeable. An emerald-green hue is more valued than yellowish green or greenish yellow. Saturated green colors are priced much higher than brownish or grayish colors.

Demantoid is typically eye-clean. Curiously, stones that have radiating fibers that look like horsetails (fig. 12.13 & 12.14) are more valued than those without them. These inclusions identify it as a natural demantoid because "horsetails" are not found in other green stones. In addition, "horsetails" suggest the stone is from Russia, a historical source noted for its fine quality demantoid. The deposits in Russia are also more likely to produce the greatest chromium content, which in turn, results in the finest colors. Some locations such as Namibia produce demantoids without horsetail inclusions. The appearance of a perfectly formed horsetail in the center of a gem-quality demantoid can increase its value by twofold, particularly if the inclusion is not obvious to the naked eye.

Fig. 12.13 Horsetail inclusion, *Demantoid: Pala Gems International; photo: Jason Stephenson.*

Fig. 12.14 Horsetail inclusion in demantoid. *Photo: GAAJ-Zenhokyo Laboratory.*

Stones that are cloudy or fractured sell for much less than those with good clarity and transparency.

As with all stones, the quality of the cut is important because it can improve the color, brilliance and dispersion of the stone.

For more detailed information on demantoid, read the article entitled "Russian Demantoid, Czar of the Garnet Family" in the summer 1996 issue of *Gems & Gemology* (100-111).

Fig. 12.15 Melanite earrings. *Design © by Eve J. Alfillé; photo by Matthew Arden.*

Fig. 12.16 Melanite ring. *Design © Eve J. Alfillé; photo by Matthew Arden.*

Melanite

Melanite is a titanium-rich variety of andradite, whose color ranges from black to dark-red. Its name originates from the Greek *melanos* meaning black or dark. Used commercially as an abrasive, it is sometimes mounted in jewelry (figs. 12.15 & 12.16). Melanite is found in several localities including Brazil, Namibia, Kenya, Italy, Germany, Austria, Czech Republic, Sweden, Norway and in the U.S. states of Alaska, Washington, California, Colorado and New Jersey. Prices for loose melanites are low—less than five dollars a carat. More often than not, it is sold by the piece or in crystalline form.

Topazolite

Topazolite is named after its similarity in color and transparency to yellow topaz. Opinions differ as to where the dividing line is between topazolite and demantoid. For example, the *GIA Gem Reference Guide* describes topazolite as a transparent to translucent yellow andradite, which may show chatoyancy.

In his book *Color Encyclopedia of Gemstones*, Joel Arem states that "topazolite from Italy is yellowish-green; demantoid is rich green, colored by Cr [chromium]."

In *Minerals and Precious Stones of Brazil*, Carlos Cornejo and Andrea Bartorelli say "topazolite or yellow andradite appears in small crystals of brownish yellow color similar to that of the yellow topaz from where the name originates."

Topazolite is so rare, that the average appraiser will never see it. If in doubt about a varietal name, the species name together with a color description is a safe way to describe a gemstone; for example, "greenish-yellow andradite." And if the species name is not known, the stone could simply be identified as a greenish-yellow garnet.

Topazolite has been found in Italy, Austria, Russia, Madagascar, China, and in the U.S. states of Arizona and California.

Fig. 12.17 Layer-like iridescence on a crystal face of a garnet from Sonora, Mexico. *Photo by Anthony de Goutière.*

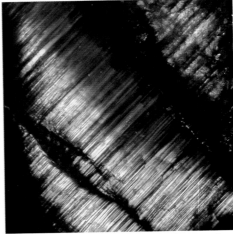

Fig. 12.18 Iridescent pattern seen in an andradite from Hermosillo, Mexico. *Pala Gems International; photo by Wimon Manorotkul.*

Rainbow Garnet

The name "rainbow garnet" comes from the iridescent effect seen on the surface of some andradite. This phenomenon is caused by lamellar (thin layered) structures within the andradite, which cause thin-film interference and probably diffraction of light.

Depending on the specimen, rainbow garnet may be either a variety of andradite or of grossular-andradite (an intermediate composition that may be called grandite). Rainbow garnet was first discovered in 1934 at the Adelaide mine, in Nevada, USA. However, because of its low quality, it was not marketed. More attractive rainbow garnet from Sonora, Mexico made its way onto the market in the late 1980's (fig.12.19), but its output was low and most of the production ceased after a few years.

Fig. 12.19 Iridescent or rainbow garnet from Sonora, Mexico. Freeform weighs 56.08 carats, the oval with four-rayed star is 23.53 cts. *Pala Gems International; photo by Wimon Manorotkul.*

In 2004, rainbow garnet was found in Nara Prefecture, Japan. It occurs as relatively small orangy brown crystals with iridescence in almost the entire range of the spectrum. It is still being sold in small quantities. For more information, see the article entitled "The Cause of Iridescence in Rainbow Andradite from Nara, Japan" in the winter 2006 issue of *Gems & Gemology.*

Fig. 12.20 Andradite Garnet- Fort Wrangell Stikine River delta-Alaska. *Wilensky Fine Minerals specimen, Stuart Wilensky photo.*

Metaphysical Properties of Andradites

Andratite is a dynamic stone of protection and power. It is said to stimulate creativity, dissolve feelings of isolation and attract intimate encounters with others. It increases stamina, courage and strength. In terms of health benefits, *The Crystal Bible* states that andradite encourages the formation of blood, energizes the liver, and aids in the assimilation of calcium, magnesium and iron.

Melanite is said to strengthen resistance, promote honesty, and help the body adjust to medication. It has been used to help treat

Fig. 12.21 Demantoid from Jeffrey Quarry in Asbestos, Quebec. *Specimen and photo from Wright's Rock Shop.*

strokes, cancer, rheumatism and arthritis. In *The Book of Stones,* Naisha Ahsian says that "black andradite immediately connects one's life force with the fiery core of the earth, allowing one access to an almost infinite supply of energy for creative work." She also states that melanite "is a good stone to use in children's rooms to prevent nightmares, or in any instance where persistent unpleasant thoughts are causing depression, disturbances or upsets. These are excellent allies in the sick room or hospital as they prevent stray negative vibrations or entities from attaching to already weakened energetic systems."

13

Red Garnets

A rizona red garnet has one of the most unique mining crews in the world—ants. These industrious workers dig underground tunnels and in the process, push dirt and tiny garnet crystals to the surface, forming anthills. Then after a rainstorm, the garnets are picked up by the Navajo Indians, who live in the Four Corners area of Arizona bordering Colorado, New Mexico and Utah. Before 1900, the Navajos used the garnets as bullets. Besides being easily available and free, the stones had symbolic value. The Indians believed that the blood-red color helped produce fatal wounds. For many years, these garnets were advertised and sold as "Indian rubies."

Arizona anthill garnet is a variety of pyrope noted for its ruby red color, which is the result of traces of chromium in the molecular structure of the crystals. Red pyrope that is colored by chromium is called **chrome pyrope**, or anthill garnet if it is found in anthills. It often occurs in diamond mines or inside diamonds as an inclusion (figs. 13.4 & 13.5). In fact, the presence of pyrope garnets in anthills in Botswana was an important clue to the discovery of the Orapa diamond mine, the world's largest diamond mine.

Pyrope, whose name is derived from the Greek *pyropos* meaning fiery, ranges in color from brownish red to purplish red. One of the most significant sources of pyrope has been the Czech Republic, formerly Czechoslovakia. The material from there is often called Bohemian garnet. Pyrope is also mined in India, China, Australia, South Africa, Brazil, Canada and several states within the USA.

Basic pyrope data:
Chemical composition: $Mg_3Al_2(SiO_4)_3$ — magnesium aluminum silicate
RI: 1.73–1.75, SG: 3.7–3.8, Hardness: 7–7.5, Dispersion: 0.022

Almandine

Almandine is said to be the most common garnet, but gem quality almandine is extremely rare. Also called almandite, almandine was named after Alabanda in Turkey, an ancient gem cutting center. It ranges from orangish red, to red and purplish red and usually has a dark tone. Its chemical formula is $Fe_3Al_2(SiO_4)_3$, but according to *Gems* by Robert Webster, almandines in jewelry contain some of the pyrope molecule, and grossular and spessartine are also present.

Almandine is known for its needle-like inclusions, which usually intersect at 70° and 110° angles in the same plane. Needle inclusions may create a cat's-eye or star effect when the garnet is cut as a cabochon (fig. 13.7). Zircon crystals with strain halos and other crystals are also commonly seen in almandine. It has a characteristic spectrum of three strong bands in the green and yellow of the spectrum at 505 nm, 527 nm, and 575 nm.

Fig. 13.1 Almandine pendant watch from Lang Antique & Estate Jewelry. *Photo by Thomas Picarella.*

Fig. 13.2 Georgian red garnet detachable pendant from Lang Antique & Estate Jewelry. *Photo by Thomas Picarella.*

Fig. 13.3 Arizona anthill garnet. *Ring and photo from Sami Fine Jewelry.*

Fig. 13.4 Chrome pyrope in a diamond. *Photo from GAAJ-Zenhokyo Laboratory.*

Fig. 13.5 Garnet inclusion in a diamond. *Photo by Anthony de Goutière.*

Fig. 13.6 Carved garnet pendant © Eve J. Alfillé. *Photo: Matthew Arden.*

The Gem A Diploma in Gemmology Course of the British Gemmological Association states that "Since some iron is present in virtually all pyrope-almandine garnets, the characteristic 'almandine spectrum' is seen in many gems in this series. However only part of the series is called 'almandine', so it is incorrect to state that the almandine spectrum proves that a gem is 'almandine'; it certainly indicates that the almandine 'molecule' is present in the garnet, and helps to identify it as a garnet. It also enables you to distinguish the gemstone from other red stones."

India, Brazil, Tanzania, Zambia, Madagascar, Sri Lanka, Australia, the United States and Canada are important sources of almandine. Star and cat's eye almandines are found in India, Sri Lanka, and the U.S. state of Idaho.

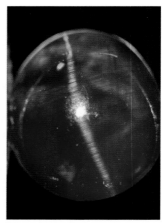

Fig. 13.7 Cat's-eye garnet.
Photo by Anthony de Goutière.

Basic almandine data:
Chemical composition: $Fe_3Al_2(SiO_4)_3$ — iron aluminum silicate
RI: 1.78–1.83, SG: 3.80–4.25, Hardness: 7.25–7.5, Dispersion: 0.024

Rhodolite and Grape Garnet®

The *Gem A Diploma in Gemmology Course* defines rhodolite as a garnet in the almandine-pyrope series with a pleasant, light purplish-red colour. The GIA *Gem Identification Lab Manual* says rhodolite is a pyrope-almandite that has a purple color component. In 1904, Max Bauer, wrote in *Precious Stones: Volume II* (pp 360-361) that rhodolite is a variety of garnet intermediate between almandine and pyrope, but more closely related to the latter. He described the color as "a pale rose-red inclining to purple like that of certain roses and rhododendrons, hence the name rhodolite." He further stated that rhodolite is a combination of two pyrope molecules with one almandine molecule with a specific gravity of 3.837 and a spectrum with absorption bands characteristic of almandine. This variety of red garnet was first described in 1898 by W. E. Hidden and J. H. Pratt. Like almandine, rhodolite may have needle-like inclusions which usually intersect at 70° and 110° angles in the same plane.

First found in North Carolina, rhodolite is now primarily mined in Tanzania, Sri Lanka, India and Mozambique.

Grape Garnet® is a trademarked name for a purple-red pyrope-almandine. According to Columbia Gem House, grape garnet is mined only in the State of Orissa on the Bay of Bengal in eastern India, and stones sold as grape garnets are eye clean and of natural color.

Basic pyrope-almandine data:
RI: 1.75–1.78, SG: 3.70–3.95, Hardness: 7-7.5, Dispersion: 0.026

Fig. 13.8 Rhodolite carved by Sherris Cottier Shank. *Photo: Amy Balthrop.*

Fig. 13.9 Rhodolite cut by John Dyer in a ring by Rebecca Paquette-Johnson. *Photo by Midge Bolt.*

Fig. 13.10 Rhodolite cut by John Dyer in a ring by Brad Weber. *Photo from Weber Goldsmith Gallery.*

Fig. 13.11 Rhodolite (6.34 cts) cut by John Dyer. *Photo by Lydia Dyer.*

Fig. 13.12 Rhodolite (7.60 cts) cut by John Dyer. *Photo by Lydia Dyer.*

Fig. 13.13 Grape garnet (3.01 ct) from Devon Fine Jewelry. *Photo: Tony Seideman.*

Fig. 13.14 Grape garnets from Columbia Gem House. *Photo © Columbia Gem House.*

Pyralspite

In Chapter 11, I stated that "pyralspite" was the series name and acronym for a group of three garnet species—pyrope, almandine and spessartine. It is also used as a varietal name for a garnet identified as pyrope-almandine-spessartine. The name is assigned by a lab on the basis of the stone's chemical composition. An example of a 51.57 ct pyralspite is shown in figure 13.15. It is remarkable that such a large stone with this composition is bright and colorful rather than dark. Its orange-red color is unusual for a garnet. As a result this stone was sold to a collector for $3000 per carat. He now owns what is probably the largest gem pyralspite ever cut.

Fig. 13.15 Pyralspite (51.75 cts) from Mayer & Watt. *Photo by Geoffrey D. Watt.*

Pricing and Evaluation of Red Garnets

High quality red garnets generally sell for less than those that are green, partly because red stones are more plentiful. In addition, many of the red garnets on the market are overly dark and have low transparency. Some of these stones sell for less than $10 per carat. You can find 1- to 5-carat red to purple commercial quality garnets for less than $100 per carat, whereas fine quality might retail for between $100–$250 per carat. High quality stones above ten carats can retail for up to $500 per carat. When a fine-quality garnet, such as the pyralspite, has a rare color, prices can go above $1000 per carat.

It doesn't matter much whether the garnet is named a pyrope, almandine, pyrope-almandine, chrome pyrope or rhodolite. What counts is its appearance, size and rarity. As I discussed in Chapter 11, if you ask two different labs to identify a red garnet, you can end up with two different names for the same stone. Hot pink, raspberry-red and orange-red or any color that is saturated and not masked by brown or gray are the most expensive colors, provided the stone is transparent, eye clean and well cut.

Don't expect to find a ruby-red garnet. Most garnets have a secondary color of purple, brown or orange. Chrome pyropes (anthill garnets) can look red if they are 6 mm or less, but when they are larger, they tend to be dark and it is difficult to see the red. Transmitted light may be necessary to bring out the red color. Look at gems under a variety of lights when buying them. Incandescent lights in a store or at a gem show can make garnets appear redder than they are in daylight. One way to lighten the color of dark red cabochon garnets is to cut them concave on the underside to let more light through the stone.

Fig. 13.16 Anthill garnet from Mayer & Watt. *Photo by Geoffrey D. Watt.*

Buyers benefit from this because they don't have to pay money for extra weight that darkens the appearance of the garnet.

Metaphysical Properties of Red Garnets

Red garnets represent love, and they encourage its expression through simple acts of kindness and compassion as well as through committed relationships. It is said that red garnets enhance sexuality and help control anger, especially towards oneself.

In *The Crystal Bible*, Judy Hall says that besides bringing deep love, almandine is a healing stone that helps with strength and stamina. She also says that almandine stimulates the eyes, treats the liver and pancreas, and helps to absorb iron in the intestines. In addition, almandine is said to increase productivity by helping one stay focused.

Hall states that pyrope bestows vitality and charisma and promotes an excellent quality of life. As for health benefits, she says that pyrope can fortify circulation, treat the digestive tract, neutralize heartburn and soothe a sore throat.

Rhodolite is said to be a warm, sincere and trusting stone that stimulates intuition and inspiration. In *The Book of Stones*, Naisha Ahsian says that rhodolite alleviates feelings of inadequacy and is a wonderful ally to call upon when one is feeling unhappy, worthless or unable to see one's way forward. She also says rhodolite helps one recover from sexually related abuse and fulfill one's life purpose by taking the appropriate steps on one's path. It's also a great stone to wear during pregnancy.

Even star garnet is noted for its spiritual powers. In *Love is in the Earth*, Melody says that star garnet "promotes connection to the other worlds, helps one to remember dreams, and helps one toward success . . . It can produce flashes of insight to assist in guiding one to 'right' and honorable endeavors."

Spessartine

Spessartine was first found at Schaffenburg in the Spessart district of Bavaria, hence the name. Until the 1990's it was a relatively rare garnet, but that has changed, thanks to discoveries of the gem in Namibia, Nigeria and Brazil

Spessartine, which has also been called spessartite, ranges in color from orange-red to orange to yellowish orange to brownish orange. Basically it is an orange garnet colored by manganese. However it usually occurs in combination with almandine, whose iron component can give spessartine a reddish color.

Basic spessartine data:
Chemical composition: $Mn_3Al_2(SiO_4)_3$ — manganese aluminum silicate
RI:1.774–1.814, SG: 3.80–4.25, Hardness: 7–7.5, Dispersion: 0.027

Fig. 14.1 Spessartines from Nigeria, Mozambique and Tanzania. *Gemstones cut by Larry Woods of Jewels by Woods; photo by John Parrish.*

Fig. 14.2 Spessartine necklace and earrings from Zaffiro. *Photo by Daniel Van Rossen.*

Fig. 14.3 Spessartine and tsavorite ring by Mark Schneider. *Photo by Robert Weldon.*

Fig. 14.4 Spessartine pendant by Zaffiro. *Photo by Daniel Van Rossen.*

Fig. 14.5 Spessartine (2.43 ct) ring by Zaffiro. *Photo by Daniel Van Rossen.*

Fig. 14.6 Spessartine briolette earrings by Zaffiro. *Photo by Daniel Van Rossen.*

Fig. 14.7 Spessartine suite from Pala Gems International. *Photo by Mia Dixon.*

Fig. 14.8 Spessartine crystal from the Navegadora mine, in Brazil. *Specimen from John S. White; photo by Isaias Casanova.*

Fig. 14.9 Spessartine crystal on albite from the Little Three Mine in Ramona, California. *Specimen from Pala Gems International; photo by Jeff Scovil.*

Geographic Sources of Spessartine

Namibia and Nigeria have been the most important producers of spessartine. For years, Namibia was noted for producing a bright tangerine-orange garnet, named **mandarin garnet**. This garnet contains small colorless fibers, which creates a velvety texture and masks dark extinction areas, making the stone appear completely orange. Unfortunately, the source of this material is exhausted. In 2007, some spessartine with a similar "mandarin" color was discovered near Loliondo, Tanzania, about 10 kilometers south of the Kenyan border. Figure 14.12 shows a spessartine crystal from this area. Nigeria is still producing spessartine, but in smaller quantities than previously.

Before the discovery of spessartine in Namibia, Nigeria and Tanzania, material from the Little Three Mine in Ramona, California was considered to be the finest quality orange garnet. In the 1990's, gem-quality spessartine from Kashmir, appeared on the market. It was called **kashmirine**, but is no longer being marketed. Spessartine has also been found in Brazil, Afghanistan, Japan, China, Madagascar, Zambia, Sri Lanka and in the U.S. states of California and Virginia. Overall, the production of spessartine has been sporadic.

Fig. 14.11 Namibian Mandarin garnet from Pala Gems International. *Photo by Wimon Manorotkul.*

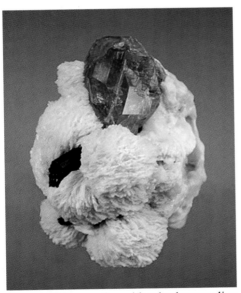

Fig. 14.10 Spessartine with schorl tourmaline and clevelandite from the Little Three mine at Ramona, San Diego County, California. *Courtesy Pala Gems International; photo by Wimon Manorotkul.*

Fig. 14.12 Mandarin color spessartine from Loliondo, Tanzania. *Specimen and photo from New Era Gems.*

Fig. 14.13 Mozambique spessartine (5.73 cts) carved by Sherris Cottier Shank. *Photo by Amy Balthrop.*

Fig. 14.14 Mandarin garnet (4.56 cts) cut by John Dyer. *Photo by Lydia Dyer.*

Fig. 14.15 Spessartines from Mayer & Watt. *Photo by Geoffrey D. Watt.*

Fig. 14.16 Spessartine (3.52 cts) cut by John Dyer. *Photo by Lydia Dyer.*

Fig. 14.14 Spessartine (11.35 cts) cut by John Dyer. *Photo by Lydia Dyer.*

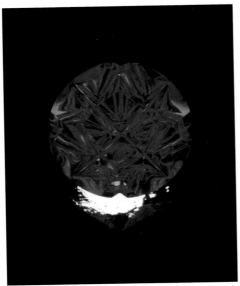

Fig. 14.5 Spessartine cut by Larry Woods of Jewels by Woods. *Photo by John Parrish.*

Fig. 14.16 Spessartine specimen from Pala Gems International. *Photo by Jeff Scovil.*

Metaphysical Properties of Spessartine

Spessartine is said to be a great help to those who are experiencing creative blocks because it stimulates all aspects of one's creative abilities and energies. In addition, it can encourage one to be more impulsive, spontaneous and intuitive. Metaphysical specialists say spessartine also:

- Enhances charisma
- Helps with weight loss
- Increases fertility
- Suppresses nightmares
- Treats lactose intolerance
- Acts as an antidepressant
- Helps cure anemia
- Encourages optimism

Pricing and Evaluation of Spessartine

In general, spessartine costs more than red garnet. Namibian mandarin garnet has fetched the highest prices—more than $2000 per carat retail in very fine quality above five carats. In sizes between one and two carats, fine quality mandarin garnet has retailed for between $500 and $800 per carat.

Commercial quality spessartine sells for less than $150 per carat. Good to high quality one-carat spessartines typically retail for between $150 and $700 per carat and larger stones up to 10 carats have retailed for between $200 and $1500 per carat.

The most valued spessartine colors are intense pure orange and red-orange. The lowest priced are yellow, pale and brownish colors. Transparency and clarity play a major role in the price. Heavily included and translucent stones are sold for prices below $25 per carat. High-quality designer-cut stones sell at premium prices.

Malaya & Color-Change Garnets

In the 1960's, miners discovered a strange reddish orange garnet while mining for rhodolite in Tanzania's Umba River Valley. When the orange stone was included in parcels of rhodolite, it was initially rejected, so African dealers started treating it as a reject garnet and nicknamed it **malaya** (also spelled malaia), which means "outcast" in Swahili. In the late 1970's, some American and German dealers saw an opportunity to market the stone. Since "Malaya" sounded exotic, they decided to keep the name.

Classified as a pyrope-spessartine garnet, malaya ranges in color from reddish orange, to pinkish orange, yellowish orange to light brown, which has also been called champagne garnet. Even though the production of malaya is small and sporadic, it is still being found along the Tanzanian and Kenyan border. The term "umbalite" has also been used for malaya, since it is from the Umba River Valley, but today **umbalite** usually refers to Tanzanian rhodolite or occasionally color-change garnet from the Umba Valley. **Imperial garnet** and **imperial malaya** are two terms used for pink or pink-orange pyrope-spessartines. The term "Imperial malaia" was used as far back as 1988 when it appeared in the Fall 98 issue of *Gems & Gemology* (p 222) to describe a brownish pinkish orange pyrope-spessartine from Madagascar. Some of the brownish material was being sold as champagne garnet.

Sometimes "imperial garnet" is used as a name for transparent pink grossular from Tanzania.

Basic pyrope-spessartine data:
RI:1.75–1.78, SG: 3.78–3.85, Hardness: 7–7.5

Fig. 15.1 Malaya garnet (6.08 cts) cut by John Dyer. *Photo by Lydia Dyer.*

Fig. 15.2 Malaya (4.00 cts) from Pala Gems International. *Photo by Mia Dixon.*

Fig. 15.3 Malayas from Tanzania cut by Larry Woods of Jewels by Woods. *Photo: John Parrish.*

Fig. 15.4 Pyrope-spessartine (2.82 cts) sample from the Lindi region of southern Tanzania, which has been marketed as Imperial garnet. *Photo by Bear Williams of Stone Group Labs.*

Fig. 15.5 Malaya rough and photo from New Era Gems.

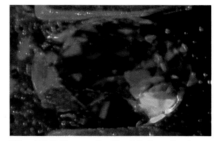

Fig. 15.6 Garnet in fig. 15.4 under long wave UV. *Photo by Bear Williams.*

Fig. 15.7 Color-change garnet cut by Larry Woods of Jewels by Woods. *Photo by John Parrish.*

Figs. 15.8 & 15.9 Color-change garnets discovered in 2009 in the Kamtonga district in Kenya shown in daylight and incandescent light (bottom). *Gems cut by Larry Woods of Jewels by Woods; photos by John Parrish.*

Fig. 15.10 Malaya carved by Sherris Cottier Shank. *Photo; Amy Balthrop.*

Fig. 15.11 Inclusions in a color-change spessartine-pyrope from Kenya. *Photo by Anthony de Goutière.*

Color-Change Garnet

Color change garnets have been reported since the 1970's, but it wasn't until their discovery in Tanzania's Umba Valley in 1987 that they became available for sale to gem collectors. In the 1990's, color-change garnet was found in Bekily in southern Madagascar. Other occurrences include the Tunduru district in Tanzania's Ruvuma region, Kenya, Sri Lanka, Russia and some parts of the USA.

The color change that occurs when viewed in daylight or fluorescent light versus incandescent light or candlelight varies depending on the stone and source. Possible color change combinations include:

♦ Yellowish green, bluish green, or forest green (daylight); purple, lavender or pink (incandescent light)
♦ Blue or green-blue (daylight); purple or lavender (incandescent light)
♦ Greenish yellow (daylight); pink (incandescent light)
♦ Orange (daylight): orangish red or purple (incandescent light)
♦ Yellow (daylight); orange (incandescent light)
♦ Brown or beige (daylight); pink (incandescent light)

The color change is usually due to traces of vanadium, but chromium is responsible for the change in some stones. Most color-change garnets are pyrope-spessartines.

There's a wide price variation among color-change garnets. Stones with a distinct color change from bluish green in daylight or florescent light to purple in incandescent light or candlelight are the most expensive with retail prices going as high as $3000 for stones above two carats. You can find brown stones and stones with little color change for less than $100. Stones between one and two carats generally range between $100 and $2000 per carat depending on their color, degree of color change, clarity, transparency, cut quality, size and rarity.

Tsavorite and Other Grossulars

Top-quality tsavorites rival emeralds in their beauty. Not only do they have a rich natural green color and higher brilliance, they also have the advantage of not needing any treatments to mask fractures and improve transparency. Tsavorite is naturally beautiful.

Most sources, say that this unique green garnet was first discovered in Tanzania in 1967 by Scottish geologist and gem prospector Campbell Bridges. However, in an historical account on www.Tsavorite.com, Bridges states that he initially discovered tsavorite in 1961 in Zimbabwe while working for the United Kingdom Atomic Energy Authority after being chased into a gully by a buffalo. His second discovery occurred in 1967 near the village of Komolo in Tanzania, but he lost the mine due to nationalization by the Tanzanian government. Bridges then decided to search for

Fig. 16.1 Tsavorite (5.62 cts) from Bear Essentials. *Photo by Robert Weldon.*

tsavorite in Kenya. Before the end of 1970, he had found his first Kenyan green garnet in the hills close to the borders of Tsavo National Park, and in 1971, he pegged the first blocks of mineral claims.

In late 1973, Henry B. Platt, then President of Tiffany & Co., who had had a keen interest in what was then called green grossularite, decided that it was time to give this gem a trade name. Traditionally most minerals ended with "ite". As Tsavo was the obvious locality choice, He and Mr. Platt named it "Tsavorite", while the Germans proposed the name "Tsavolite. CIBJO, The World Jewellery Confederation, ruled to accept the name "tsavorite."

Most tsavorite comes from the East African countries of Tanzania, Kenya and Madagascar. Minor amounts are also found in Pakistan.

Tsavorite owes its color to trace amounts of vanadium or chromium. The largest fine-color clean tsavorite is said to weigh 160.78 carats and was found near Arusha, Tanzania at the border of the original block B tanzanite mining area at a depth of 160 meters. TanzaniteOne's subsidiary company, TsavoriteOne is currently exploring for tsavorite in an area 40 km's south of the Merelani Tanzanite Mines. The exploration is currently in the bulk sampling phase. The decision to mine tsavorite will be made following the exploration.

Fig. 16.2 Tsavorite earrings by Erica Courtney. *Photo from TsavoriteOne.*

Fig. 16.3 Tsavorite pendant from Omi Gems. *Photo by Diamond Graphics.*

Fig. 16.4 Woman's tsavorite ring by Hubert Inc. *Photo by Diamond Graphics.*

Fig. 16.5 Gent's tsavorite ring made and photographed by Michael Jakubowski.

Fig. 16.6 Tsavorite ring from Devon Fine Jewelry. *Photo by Tony Seideman.*

Fig. 16.7 Tsavorite ring from Omi Gems. *Photo by Diamond Graphics.*

Fig. 16.8 Tsavorite and diamond ring from Lang Antique & Estate Jewelry. *Photo by Thomas Picarella.*

Fig. 16.9 Tsavorite accented with diamonds and green, brown & yellow enamel. *Pendant and photo from Timeless Gems.*

Fig. 16.10 Tsavorite necklace from Lang Antique & Estate Jewelry. *Photo by Thomas Picarella.*

Fig. 16.11 Merelani mint garnet (1.74 cts) and photo from New Era Gems.

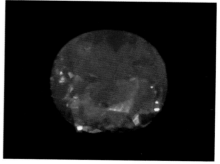

Figs 16.12 & 16.13 A Tanzanian tsavorite under normal lighting and UV lighting (396 nm UV LED). Most garnets, including tsavorites from Kenya, are usually inert to UV light, but a few grossulars fluoresce. *Photos by Bear Williams of Stone Group Laboratories.*

Tsavorite is the most expensive grossular. In sizes above five carats, fine quality stones can retail for up to $8000 per carat. Between two to five carats, gem quality stones range between $3000 and $5000 per carat retail. Most tsavorites are under two carat and high quality stones retail for between $1,500 and $4,000 per carat. Commercial quality between one and two carats ranges between about $200 and $700 per carat. Low quality stones can be found for less.

An intense emerald green is the most valued. Overly dark, yellowish green or brownish green stones sell for significantly less. Light green stones are usually classified as green grossular, rather than tsavorite and their cost is significantly less than tsavorite. The clarity of tsavorite is usually fairly good; therefore, try to find eye-clean stones.

Grossular is found in a variety of colors, which will be described in the rest of this chapter. Its name originates from the botanical name for the gooseberry, *grossularia*, which displays a green color common to some grossulars.

Basic grossular data:
Chemical composition: $Ca_3Al_2(SiO_4)_3$ — calcium aluminum silicate
RI: 1.73–1.75, SG: 3.4–3.8, Hardness: 6.75–7.25, Dispersion: 0.028

Mint Garnet

Mint garnet is a light green grossular with a hint of blue (fig. 16.11). It was first discovered around 1998 in the same area as tanzanite—the Merelani Hills in the Arusha region of Tanzania. As a result it is often referred to as "Merelani mint." Some use the term "mint garnet" to apply to any green grossular from any source, but technically it should be a slightly bluish green in color. Mint garnet tends to be more included than tsavorite, but eye-clean stones are available.

Hessonite or Grossular

Unlike tsavorite and mint garnet, hessonite has been known for centuries. Both the ancient Greeks and Romans made cameos and cabochons with hessonite. The name comes from the Greek word *hesson*. meaning inferior, because it is less dense and slightly softer than some other garnets. Hessonite ranges in color from yellow to orange to brown and is sometimes called cinnamon stone because of its orange-brown color, which is caused by a combination of iron and manganese.

Sri Lanka is an important source of hessonite. It is also found in India, Madagascar, Kenya, Tanzania, Mexico, Brazil, Russia, the province of Quebec in Canada, and the U.S. states of California, Maine and New Hampshire. It usually retails for less than $100 a carat.

Figs. 16.14–16.16 Left to right: Hessonnites from Madagascar, Tanzania and Quebec. *Hessonites cut & photographed by Coast-to-Coast Rarestones International.*

Fig. 16.17 Asscher-cut grossular from J. L. White Fine Gemstones. *Photo by Jeff White.*

Fig. 16.18 Transparent green grossular from Omi Gems. *Photo by Diamond Graphics.*

Fig. 16.19 Grossular from Tanzania (6.83 cts). *Pala Gems International. Photo: Mia Dixon.*

Fig. 16.20 Grossular (23.21 cts) from *Pala Gems International. Photo by Mia Dixon.*

Fig. 16.21 Hydrogrossular carved by Sherris Cottier Shank. *Photo by Amy Balthrop.*

Fig. 16.22 Hydrogrossular sculpture by Sherris Cottier Shank. *Photo by Amy Balthrop.*

Most hessonite is too included to use in jewelry. It often contains masses of crystal inclusions such as apatite, diopside and zircon, which give it a "heat wave" or "scotch-in-water" effect that is characteristic of hessonite.

Some yellow, orange or greenish yellow grossular is transparent and does not have the characteristic inclusions found in hessonite (fig. 16.17). These garnets are simply called grossulars or grossularites and sell at higher prices than hessonite because of their higher quality. Grossular may also be colorless.

Green Grossular or Hydrogrossular

If green grossular is translucent, semi-opaque or too light to be called tsavorite, it is simply called green grossular or grossular. Massive (rocklike) grossular is also identified as hydrogrossular; it may contain up to 5% water and can be found in large boulders. The green variety has erroneously been called garnet jade because of its resemblance to jade. In South Africa, one of the main areas where it is found, it is sometimes sold as Transvaal jade or South African jade. The material is used for beads and cabochons and typically sells for less than $10 a carat. Strands of green hydrogrossular generally retail for less than $100. Light colored transparent green or greenish yellow grossular costs more, but can usually be found for less than $200 per carat although fine-quality stones above five carats can retail for up to $500 per carat.

Basic hydrogrossular data:
Composition: $(OH),Ca_3Al_2(SiO_4)_3$ — calcium aluminum silicate with hydroxide
RI: 1.70–1.73, SG: 3.3–3.6, Hardness: 6.75–7.25

Pink Hydrogrossular and Grossular

Colored by iron, pink hydrogrossular is translucent to semiopaque and occurs in South Africa and Mexico (fig. 16.21). The Mexican material is known as rosolite. Prices are low—less than $10 per carat, and sometimes it is simply sold by the piece or as a specimen.

Transparent pink grossular (fig. 16.19) is found in Tanzania and is sometimes called **imperial garnet**, which is confusing because pyrope-spessartine from Tanzania may also be referred to as imperial garnet. Whether material is called imperial garnet or pink grossular, it is still priced the same, which can be a few hundred dollars per carat for top quality material. Low grade material, sells for much less. It is difficult to locate transparent pink grossular, no matter what the quality.

Leuco Garnet

Transparent colorless grossular is called **leuco garnet**. Its hydrogrossular counterpart is white and translucent. Quite often, material that appears colorless is actually an extremely light green or yellow. Leuco garnet usually sells for less than $100 per carat, whereas white hydrogrossular sells for less than $10 a carat or is sold by the piece.

Fig. 16.23 Grossular from Tanzania courtesy Coast-to-Coast Rarestones Intl.

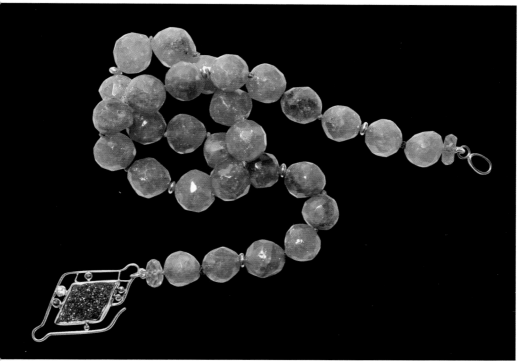

Fig. 16.24 Grossular garnets in their natural crystal form, resembling gooseberries, and a drusy uvarovite from Russia. *Necklace design © Eve Alfillé; photo by Matthew Arden.*

Mali Garnet

Mali garnet is a transparent grossular-andradite hybrid, which is mined in the Republic of Mali, a landlocked country in western Africa. The stone, which ranges in color from yellow to greenish yellow to brown, is sometimes called "grandite," an acronym of "grossular" and andradite."

One year after its discovery in 1994, large amounts of Mali garnet were produced, bringing its price down. In recent years, much smaller amounts have been produced and prices have risen. High-quality Mali garnets in the one- to two-carat range retail for between $150–$500 per carat; commercial quality stones can be found for less than $50 per carat, with brown colors being priced the lowest. As large size rough is rare in this variety, price per carat increases dramatically with size. Very fine quality Mali garnets weighing more than five carats can retail for up to $1500 per carat.

In the fall 1998 issue of *Gems & Gemology* (pp 221, 222), the GIA noted that some Mali garnets are grossulars rather than grossular-andradite."

Basic grossular-andradite data:

RI: 1.762–1.779, Orange to brown stones generally have higher RIs than yellowish green or green stones, SG: 3.64–3.68, Hardness: 6.75–7

Fig. 16.25 Mali garnet (7.53 cts) cut by John Dyer. *Photo by Lydia Dyer.*

Fig. 16.26 Mali garnet (3.02 cts) cut by John Dyer. *Photo by Lydia Dyer.*

Fig. 16.27 Grandite (5.37 cts) from *Pala Gems International. Photo by Mia Dixon.*

Fig. 16.28 Mali garnet specimen and photo from New Era Gems.

Fig. 16.29 Grossular-Jeffrey Quarry, Asbestos, Quebec, Canada. *Wilensky Fine Minerals specimen, Stuart Wilensky photo.*

Fig. 16.30 Grossular-Jeffrey Quarry, Asbestos, Quebec, Canada. *Wilensky Fine Minerals specimen, Stuart Wilensky photo.*

Fig. 16.31 Mali garnet (2.76 cts) cut by John Dyer. *Photo by Lydia Dyer.*

Fig. 16.32 Mali garnet (1.28 cts) cut by John Dyer. *Photo by Lydia Dyer.*

Metaphysical Properties of Grossular

The Egyptians believed that grossular protects against crime, cures inflammation, cleanses the blood and strengthens bones. In *The Crystal Bible*, Judy Hall says that grossular is a useful stone to have during challenges and lawsuits because it helps one to relax and go with the flow. Hall also states that grossular enhances fertility, aids in the assimilation of vitamin A, relieves arthritis, fortifies the kidneys and benefits the mucus membranes and skin.

Vedic astrologers believe that when set in gold, hessonite is a powerful talisman that increases life span and happiness. Hessonite elixir has been used for the liver, skin, bones, nightmares and psychosomatic illness. *The Crystal Bible* says that hessonite eliminates feelings of guilt and inferiority, opens the intuition and psychic abilities, regulates hormone production, and reduces infertility and impotence. When used for out-of-body journeys, hessonite can carry the participant to his or her destination.

Robert Simmons, in *The Book of Stones*, says that tsavorite represents true wealth in all its positive aspects— financial, creative, emotional, and even physical health. In addition, tsavorites enhance vitality, increase zest for living, and induce feelings of charity, and benevolence. "In their gem form, he explains, tsavorites can transmit their beneficial qualities through the eyes of those who behold them. In work situations, wearing a tsavorite can 'infect' one's coworkers, or one's entire company with its optimistic, prosperous vibrations, and that can be helpful for everyone."

Fig. 16.33 Tsavorite from Omi Gems. *Photo by Diamond Graphics.*

Appendix: Where to Find an Appraiser

Several people have asked me for recommendations for jewelry and gem appraisers, so I created a list of independent appraisers who are gemologists and who have completed formal education in appraisal procedures, ethics and law. You can find it on my website www.reneenewman.com by clicking on the "appraisers" link, or you can go directly to the appraisers' page at http://reneenewman.com/appraisers.htm. Because I haven't met all of these appraisers, this list is not an endorsement; it's just for your convenience.

There are also highly qualified appraisers who work in jewelry stores. You can locate them and independent appraisers as well by contacting the following organizations:

American Society of Appraisers (ASA)
555 Herndon Parkway, Suite 125, Herndon, VA 20170
Phone (703) 478-2228, FAX (703) 742-8471, http://www.appraisers.org

Canadian Jeweller's Institute
27 Queen St. East, Suite 600, Toronto, Ontario M5C 2M6 Canada
Phone (416) 368-7616 ext 223 Fax (416) 368-1986
http://www.canadianjewellers.com/html/aapmemberlist.htm

International Society of Appraisers (ISA)
737 N. Michigan Ave. Suite 2100, Chicago, IL 60611
Phone (312) 981-6778 Fax (312) 981-6787, http://www.isa-appraisers.org

National Association of Jewelry Appraisers (NAJA)
P.O. Box 18, Rego Park, New York, 11374-0018
Phone (718) 896-1536, http://www.NAJAappraisers.org

Value the Past (An appraisal service that specializes in antique and estate jewelry and personal property)
Phone (877) 797-9011, Fax (866) 551-5017, http://www.valuethepast.com

In Australia, you can find appraisers through the following branches of the National Council of Jewelry Valuers:

NCJV Inc. (National Council of Jewelry Valuers)
Sydney, New South Wales, Australia
Phone 02 9232 6599   FAX 02 9232 6399,   http://www.ncjv.com.au/

NCJV Inc. (Queensland)
Grange, Queensland, Australia
Phone/Fax 07 3857 4377 Email: qld@ncjv.com.au

NCJV Inc. (South Australia Division)
Henley Beach, South Australia, Australia
Phone 08 8234 2505 Fax 08 8125 5822 Email: sa@ncjv.com.au

NCJV Inc. (Tasmania Division)
Hobart, Tasmania, Australia
Phone 03 6234 2426 Fax 03 6231 5366 Email: tas@ncjv.com.au

NCJV Inc., (Victoria Division)
Melbourne VIC Australia
Phone 03 9500 9250 Fax 03 9500 2904 Email: vic@ncjv.com.au

NCJV Inc., Western Australia, Australia
Perth WA Australia
Phone 08 9409 2009 Fax 08 9364 5504 Email: wa@ncjv.com.au

After you get the names of some appraisers, you'll need to interview them to find out if they are qualified to appraise your jewelry. When interviewing an appraiser you should ask:

♦ What are your qualifications? Basic information about gemological and appraisal credentials is provided on my website at http://reneenewman.com/qa.htm.
♦ How much do you charge?
♦ What does your appraisal fee include? The last chapter of Volume 1 of Exotic Gems outlines what a good appraisal includes. More detailed appraisal information is also available in my *Gem & Jewelry Pocket Guide* and *Ruby, Sapphire & Emerald Buying Guide.*
♦ What experience do you have in valuing the items requiring an appraisal? For example, if you have period jewelry (Art Deco, Art Nouveau, Victorian, etc.), the appraiser should know the market for it in order for you to obtain an accurate value. The same is true for colored stones. It's fairly straightforward to appraise contemporary jewelry with diamonds, but other types of jewelry may require specialized experience.

A good interview can provide information you'll need to select an experienced and ethical appraiser who provides thorough and accurate appraisals.

Bibliography

Books & Booklets

Ahrens, Joan & Malloy, Ruth. *Hong Kong Gems & Jewelry*. Hong Kong: Delta Dragon, 1986.

Anderson, B. W. *Gem Testing*. Verplanck, NY: Emerson Books, 1985.

Arem, Joel. *Color Encyclopedia of Gemstones*. New York: Chapman & Hall, 1987.

Bauer, Jaroslav & Bouska, Vladimir. *Pierres Precieuses et Pierres Fines*. Paris: Bordas, 1985.

Bauer, Dr. Max. *Precious Stones Volume II*. New York: Dover Publications: 1968, English translation first published in 1904.

Bonewitz, Ronald. *Rock & Gem*. New York: Dorling Kindersley Ltd., 2008.

Butler, Gail, *Crystal & Gemstone Divination*. Baldwin Park, CA: Gem Guides Book Co. 2008.

Ciprani, Curzio & Borelli, Alessandro. *Simon & Schuster's Guide to Gems and Precious Stones*. New York: Simon and Schuster, 1986

Cody, Andrew. *Australian Precious Opal*. Melbourne. Andrew Cody Party Ltd. 1991.

Collings, Michael R. *GemLore Second Edition*. Marland: Wildside Press, 2009.

Cornejo, Carlos & Barorelli, Andrea. *Minerals & Precious Stones of Brazil*. Sau Paulo: Solaris Cultural Publications, 2009.

Cram, Len. *Beautiful Opals Auttralia's National Gem*. Lightning Ridge: Len Cram, 1999.

Crowe, Judith. *The Jeweler's Directory of Gemstones*. Buffalo, NY: Firefly Books, 2006.

Downing, Paul. *Opal Identification and Value*. Tallahassee: Majextic Press. 1992.

Duysters, George F. *Opals from a Mexican Mine*. New Amsterdam Book Company, 1896.

Eason, Cassandra. *The Illustrated Directory of Healing Crystals*. London: Collins & Brown, 2004.

Eckert, Allan. *The World of Opals*. New York: John Wiley & Sons, Inc., 1997.

ExtraLapis No. 9, *Opal the Phenomenal Gemstone*. East Hampton, CT: Lithographic, LLC. 2007.
ExtraLapis No. 11, *Garnet: Great Balls of Fire*. East Hampton, CT: Lithographic, LLC. 2008.

Federman, David & Hammid, Tino. *Consumer Guide to Colored Gemstones*. Shawnee Mission, Modern Jeweler, 1989.

Gemological Institute of America. *Gem Reference Guide*. Santa Monica, CA: GIA, 1988.

Grande, Lance, & Augustyn, Allison. *Gems & Gemstones*. Chicago: Univ. of Chicago Press, 2009.

Gubelin, Eduard J. *The Color Treasury of Gemstones*. New York: Thomas Y. Crowell, 1984.

Gubelin, Eduard J. & Koivula, John I. *Photoatlas of Inclusions in Gemstones, Volume 2*. Basel: Opinio Publishers, 2005.

Gubelin, Eduard J. & Koivula, John I. *Photoatlas of Inclusions in Gemstones*. Zurich: ABC Edition, 1986.

Hall, Cally. *Eyewitness Handbooks, Gemstones*. London: Dorling Kindersley, 1994.

Hall, Judy, *Crystal Bible*. Cincinnatti: Walking Stick Press, 2004.

Hall, Judy. *Illustrated Guide to Crystals*. New York: Sterling, 2000.

Hanneman, William, *Naming Gem Garnets*. Hanneman Gemmolgical Instruments, 2000.

Hodgkinson, Alan. *Visual Optics, Diamond and Gem Identification Without Instruments*. Northbrook, IL: Gemworld International, Inc., 1995.

HRD, *Gemmology Basic Course*, Antwerp, HRD, 2005.

Hurlbut, Cornelius. *Dana's Manual of Mineralogy*. New York: John Wiley & Sons, 1971.

Jewelers of America. *The Gemstone Enhancement Manual*. New York: Jewelers of America, 2005.

Keller, Peter. *Gemstones of East Africa*. Phoenix: Geoscience Press Inc., 1992.

Kunz, George Frederick. *The Curious Lore of Precious Stones*. New York: Bell, 1989.

Kunz, George Frederick. *Gems & Precious Stones of North America*. New York: Dover, 1968.

Leechman, Frank. *The Opal Book*. Sydney: Ure Smith Publishers, 1969.

Liddicoat, Richard T. *Handbook of Gem Identification*. Santa Monica, CA: GIA, 1989.

Melody. *Love is the Earth, A Kaleidoscope of Crystals*. Wheat Ridge, CO: Earth-Love Publishing House, 1995.

Nassau, Kurt. *Gems Made by Man*. Santa Monica, CA: Gemological Institute of America, 1980.

Nassau, Kurt. *Gemstone Enhancement, Second Edition*. London: Butterworths, 1994.

Newman, Renée. *Exotic Gems: Volume 1,*. Los Angeles: Intl. Jewelry Publ., 2010.

Newman, Renée. *Gemstone Buying Guide*. Los Angeles: Intl. Jewelry Publications, 2008.

O'Donoghue, Michael, Joyner Louise. *Identification of Gemstones*. Oxford, Butterworth Heinemann, 2003.

O'Donoghue, Michael. *Identifying Man-made Gems*. London: N.A.G. Press, 1983.

O'Donoghue, Michael. *Synthetic, Imitation & Treated Gemstones*. Oxford: Butterworth-Heinemann, 1997.

O'Leary, Barry. *A Field Guide to Australian Opals*. Melbourne, Gemcraft Books, 1977

O'Leary, Barry. *L'Opale: Mythe et Fascination*, Paris. Publigemme International, 1984

Perry, Nance and Ron. *Australian Opals in Colour*. Sydney: A. H. & A. W. Reed, 1069.

Peschek-Bohmer, Schreiber, Gisela. *Healing Crystals and Gemstones*. Munich, Koneckky & Konecky, 2003.

Pough, Frederick. *Peterson Field Guides, Rocks and Minerals*. Boston: Houghton Miffln , 1983.

Read, Peter G. *Gemmology*. Oxford: Butterworth-Heineman, 1996.

Rouse, John. *Garnet*. London: Butterworth's Gem Books, 1986.

Rubin, Howard & Levine. Gail, *GemDialogue Color Tool Box*. Rego Park, NY, GemDialogue Systems, Inc., 1997.

Rubin, Howard. *Grading & Pricing with GemDialogue*. New York: GemDialogue Co., 1986.

Schmetzer, Karl. *Russian Alexandrites*. Stuttgart: Schweizerbart Science Publishers, 2010.

Schumann, Walter. *Gemstones of the World*. New York: Sterling, 1997.

Simmons, Robert & N. Ahsian. *Book of Stones.* Montpelier, VT: Heaven & Earth Publishing, 2005.

Sinkankas, John. *Gem Cutting: A Lapidary's Manual.* New York: Van Nostrand Reinhold, 1962.

Sinkankas, John. *Van Nostrand's Standard Catalogue of Gems.* New York: Van Nostrand Reinhold, 1968.

Sinkankas, John. *Gemstone & Mineral Data Book.* Prescott, AZ. Geoscience Press, 1988.

Skuratowicz, Arthur & Nash, Julie. *Working with Gemstones, a Bench Jeweeler's Guide.* Providence: MJSA/AJM Press, 2005.

Smith, G. F. Herbert. *Gemstones.* London, Methuen & Co. Ltd. 1949.

Sofianides, Anna & Harlow, George. *Gems & Crystals from the American Museum of Natural History.* New York: Simon & Shuster, 1990.

Streeter, Edwin W. *Precious Stones and Gems, Their History, Sources and Characteristics.* London: G. Bell & Sons, 1898.

Suwa, Yasukazu. *Gemstones Quality & Value (English Edition).* GIA and Suwa & Son, Inc., 1994.

Thomas, Arthur. *The Gemstones Handbook.* UK: New Holland Publishers, 2008.

Varley, E. R. *Sillimanite: Andalusite, Kyanite, Sillimanite.* New York: Chemical Publishing Co. 1968

Webster, Robert. *Gemmologists' Compendium.* New York: Van Nostrand Reinhold, 1979.

Webster, Robert. *Gems, Fourth Edition.* London, Butterworths,1983.

Webster, Robert. *Practical Gemmology.* Ipswich, Suffolk: N. A. G. Press, 1976.

White, John S. *The Smithsonian Treasury Minerals and Gems.* Washington D.C.: Smithsonian Institution Press, 1991.

Wise, Richard. *Secrets of the Gem Trade.* Lenox, MA: Brunswick House Press, 2003.

Periodicals

Auction Market Resource for Gems & Jewelry. P. O. Box 7683 Rego Park, NY, 11374.

Australian Gemmologist. Brisbane: Gemmological Association of Australia

Canadian Gemmologist. Toronto: Canadian Gemmological Association.

Colored Stone. Malverne, PA: Colored Stone.

Gem & Jewellery News. London. Gemmological Association and Gem Testing Laboratory of Great Britain.

Gems and Gemology. Santa Monica, CA: Gemological Institute of America.

The GemGuide. Glenview, IL: Gemworld International, Inc.

InColor: New York, ICA (International Colored Gemstone Association)

Jewellery Business. Richmond Hill, ON, Kenilworth Media, Inc.

Jewelers Circular Keystone. Radnor, PA: Chilton Publishing Co.

JQ Magazine. San Francisco, GQ publishing..

Jewelry News Asia. Hong Kong, CMP Asia Ltd.

Jewellery Review. Hong Kong, Brilliant Art Group.

Journal of Gemmology, London: Gemmological Association and Gem Testing Laboratory of Great Britain.

Lapidary Journal Jewelry Artist. Interweave Press.

Michelsen Gemstone Index. Port Angeles, WA.

Mineralogical Record. Tucson, AZ: Mineralogical Record, Inc.

Modern Jeweler. Melville, NY: Cygnus Publishing Inc.

National Jeweler. New York: National Business Media.

Palmieri's Auction/FMV Monitor. New York, NY: GCAL

Rock & Gem. Ventura, CA, Miller Magazines, Inc.

Rocks & Minerals. Philadelphia: Taylor and Francis Group.

Southern Jewelry News. Greensboro, NC., *Southern Jewelry News.*

Miscellaneous: Courses, Notes, Leaflets, & Theses

Alatorre, Juan José Virgen. *Magdalena, Famosa Tierra de Opalos.* Centro Universitario de los Valles, 2008.

Beesley, C. R., *AGL Training Manual*

Gem A Diploma in Gemmology Course, 2009.

Gemological Institute of America Appraisal Seminar Handbook.

Gemological Institute of America Gem Identification Course.

Gemological Institute of America Gem Identification Lab Manual

Gemological Institute of America Colored Stone Grading Course.

Gemological Institute of America Colored Stone Grading Course Charts.

Gemological Institute of America Colored Stones Course

Ramirez, Carmen. *The Mexican Opal.* Canadian Institute of Gemmology, 1995.

Index

Other Books by RENÉE NEWMAN
Graduate Gemologist (GIA)

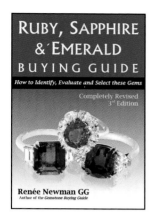

Ruby, Sapphire & Emerald Buying Guide

How to Identify, Evaluate & Select these Gems

An advanced, full-color guide to identifying and evaluating rubies, sapphires and emeralds including information on treatments, grading systems, geographic sources, fakes, synthetics, lab reports, appraisals, and gem care.

"**Enjoyable reading . . . profusely illustrated with color photographs** showing not only the beauty of finished jewelry but close-ups and magnification of details such as finish, flaws and fakes . . . Sophisticated enough for professionals to use . . . highly recommended . . . **Newman's guides are the ones to take along when shopping**." *Library Journal*

"**Solid, informative and comprehensive** . . . dissects each aspect of ruby and sapphire value in detail . . . a wealth of grading information . . . a definite thumbs-up!"
  C. R. Beesley, President, American Gemological Laboratories, *JCK Magazine*

187 pages, 280 photos, 267 in color, 6" by 9", ISBN 978-0929975-41-2, US$19.95

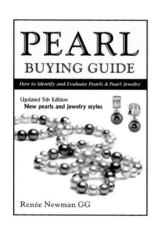

Pearl Buying Guide

How to Evaluate, Identify, Select and Care for Pearls & Pearl Jewelry

"**Copious color photographs** . . . explains how to appraise and distinguish among all varieties of pearls . . . takes potential buyers and collectors through the ins and outs of the pearl world." *Publisher's Weekly*

"**An indispensable guide** to judging [pearl] characteristics, distinguishing genuine from imitation, and making wise choices . . . useful to all types of readers, from the professional jeweler to the average patron . . . **highly recommended**." *Library Journal*

"A **well written, beautifully illustrated** book designed to help retail customers, jewelry designers, and store buyers make informed buying decisions about the various types of pearls and pearl jewelry." *Gems & Gemology*

154 pages, 321 photos (207 are new), 6" by 9", ISBN 978-0929975-44-3, US$19.95

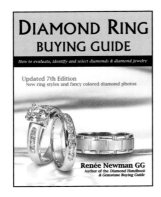

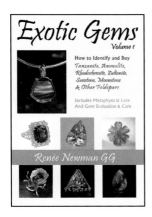

Exotic Gems, Volume 1

This is the first in a series of books that explores the history, lore, evaluation, geographic sources, and identifying properties of lesser-known gems. *Exotic Gems, Volume 1* has detailed info and close-up color photos of mounted and loose tanzanite, labradorite, zultanite, rhodochrosite, sunstone, moonstone, ammolite, spectrolite, amazonite andesine, bytownite, orthoclase and oligoclase.

"Chapters including 'Price factors in a nutshell' will prove indispensable to novice buyers. The breadth of information on each stone, Renee's guide to choosing an appraiser, 288 vibrant photos and a bibliography also make this book a handy resource for seasoned collectors. We'll be watching for future installments of the *Exotic Gems* series." *Bead & Button*

". . . contains many many color photographs that cover the spectrum of subjects from mining locality shots to cutting to subtle color variations to the finished jewelry, as appropriate . . . A quick glance at the acknowledgments shows that a great deal of networking and editorial effort has gone into this book. If you want to buy one of the materials covered by this book, already have spent your money but want an appraisal, or are just plain interested in zultanite, I highly recommend *Exotic Gems Volume 1*."

Rocks & Minerals

154 pages, 288 color photos, 6" x 9", ISBN 978-0-929975-42-9, US$19.95

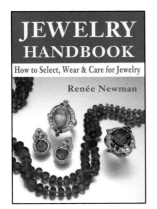

Jewelry Handbook
How to Select, Wear & Care for Jewelry

The *Jewelry Handbook* is like a Jewelry 101 course on the fundamentals of jewelry metals, settings, finishes, necklaces, chains, clasps, bracelets, rings, earrings, brooches, pins, clips, manufacturing methods and jewelry selection and care. It outlines the benefits and drawbacks of the various setting styles, mountings, chains, and metals such as gold, silver, platinum, palladium, titanium, stainless steel and tungsten. It also provides info and color photos on gemstones and fineness marks and helps you select versatile, durable jewelry that flatters your features.

"A great introduction to jewellery and should be required reading for all in the industry." Dr. Jack Ogden, CEO Gem-A (British Gemmological Association)

"A user-friendly, beautifully illustrated guide, allowing for quick reference to specific topics." *The Jewelry Appraiser*

"Valuable advice for consumers and the trade, specifically those in retail sales and perhaps even more for jewelry appraisers . . . An easy read and easy to find valuable lists and details." Richard Drucker GG, *Gem Market News*

177 pages, 297 color & 47 b/w photos, 6" x 9", ISBN 978-0-929975-38-2, US$19.95

Other Books by RENÉE NEWMAN

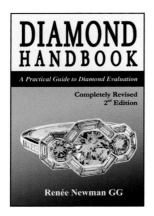

Diamond Handbook
A Practical Guide to Diamond Evaluation

Updates professionals on new developments in the diamond industry and provides advanced information on diamond grading, treatments, synthetic diamonds, fluorescence, and fancy colored diamonds. It also covers topics not in the *Diamond Ring Buying Guide* such as diamond grading reports, light performance, branded diamonds, diamond recutting, and antique diamond cuts and jewelry.

"**Impressively comprehensive**. . . . a **practical, well-organized and concisely written** volume, packed with valuable information. The *Diamond Handbook* is destined to become an indispensable reference for the consumer and trade professional alike." *Canadian Gemmologist*

"The text covers everything the buyer needs to know, with useful comments on lighting and first-class images. No other text in current circulation discusses recutting and its possible effects ... **This is a must for anyone buying, testing or valuing a polished diamond and for students in many fields.**" *Journal of Gemmology*

186 pages, 320 photos (most in color), 6" x 9", ISBN 978-0-929975-39-9, US$19.95

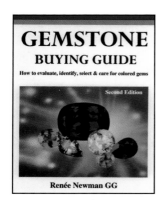

Gemstone Buying Guide
How to Evaluate, Identify and Select Colored Gems

"Praiseworthy, **a beautiful gem-pictorial reference** and a help to everyone in viewing colored stones as a gemologist or gem dealer would. . . . One of the finest collections of gem photographs I've ever seen ... If you see the book, you will probably purchase it on the spot." *Anglic Gemcutter*

"**A quality Buying Guide** that is recommended for purchase to consumers, gemmologists and students of gemmology—irrespective of their standard of knowledge of gemmology. The information is comprehensive, factual, and well presented. Particularly noteworthy in this book are the quality colour photographs that have been carefully chosen to illustrate the text. *Australian Gemmologist*

"**Beautifully produced**. . . . With colour on almost every opening few could resist this book whether or not they were in the gem and jewellery trade." *Journal of Gemmology*

156 pages, 281 color photos, 7" X 9", ISBN 978-0929975-34-4, US$19.95

Osteoporosis Prevention

" . . . a complete, practical, and easy-to-read reference for osteoporosis prevention . . . As the founding president of the Taiwan Osteoporosis Association, I am delighted to recommend this book to you."

Dr. Ko-En Huang, Founding President of TOA

"The author, Renée Newman has abundant experience in translating technical terms into everyday English. She writes this book about osteoporosis prevention from a patient's perspective. These two elements contribute to **an easy-to-read and understandable book for the public. To the medical professions, this is also a very valuable reference**."

Dr. Chyi-Her Lin, Dean of Medical College, Natl Cheng Kung Univ / Taiwan

"I was impressed with the comprehensive nature of *Osteoporosis Prevention* and its use of scientific sources. . . .The fact that the author has struggled with bone loss and can talk from personal experience makes the book more interesting and easy to read. Another good feature is that the book has informative illustrations and tables, which help clarify important points. I congratulate the author for writing **a sound and thorough guide to osteoporosis prevention**."   Ronald Lawrence MD, PhD

Co-chair of the first Symposium on Osteoporosis of the National Institute on Aging

" . . . **clarifies the inaccurate concepts from the Internet**. It contains abundant information and really deserves my recommendation."

Dr. Yung-Kuei Soong, The 6th President of Taiwanese Osteoporosis Association

"The book is written from a patient's experience and her secrets to bone care. This book is **so interesting that I finished reading it the following day** . . . The author translates all the technical terms into everyday English which makes this book so easy to read and understand."

Dr. Sheng-Mou Hou, Ex-minister, Dept. of Health / Taiwan

"**A competent and thoroughly 'reader friendly' approach to preventing osteoporosis**. Inclusive of information on how to: help prevent osteoporosis and broken bones; get enough calcium and other bone nutrients from food; make exercise safe and fun; retain a youthful posture; select a bone density center; get maximum benefit from your bone density exam; understand bone density reports; help seniors maintain their muscles and their bones; and how to be a savvy patient. *Osteoporosis Prevention* should be a part of every community health center and public library Health & Medicine reference collection . . ."

Midwest Book Review

"With great interest, I have read Renée Newman's *Osteoporosis Prevention* which provides complete and practical information about osteoporosis from a patient's perspective. . . . **a must-read reference for osteoporosis prevention**."

Dr. Tzay-Shing Yang, 3rd President of TOA, President of Taiwan Menopause Care Society

You can get free information about osteoporosis prevention, bone density testing and reports at: **www.avoidboneloss.com**

176 pages, 6" X 9", ISBN 978-0929975-37-5, US$15.95

Order Form

TITLE	Price Each	Quantity	Total
Exotic Gems, Volume 2	$19.95		
Exotic Gems, Volume 1	$19.95		
Ruby, Sapphire & Emerald Buying Guide	$19.95		
Gemstone Buying Guide	$19.95		
Diamond Handbook	$19.95		
Pearl Buying Guide	$19.95		
Jewelry Handbook	$19.95		
Diamond Ring Buying Guide	$18.95		
Gem & Jewelry Pocket Guide	$11.95		
Osteoporosis Prevention	$15.95		
		Book Total	
SALES TAX for California residents only		**(book total x $.0825)**	
SHIPPING: USA: first book $4.00, each additional copy $2.00 Canada & Mexico - airmail: first book $11.00, ea. addl. $5.00 All other foreign countries - airmail: first book $14.00, ea. addl. $7.00			
TOTAL AMOUNT with tax (if applicable) and shipping (Pay foreign orders with an international money order or a check drawn on a U.S. bank.)		**TOTAL**	

Available at major book stores or by mail. For quantity orders e-mail: intljpubl@aol.com

Mail check or money order in U.S. funds

To: International Jewelry Publications
P.O. Box 13384
Los Angeles, CA 90013-0384 USA

Ship to:

Name_____

Address_____

City_____ State or Province_____

Postal or Zip Code_____ Country _____